THE NATIVE ROCK

The Geology of
Acadia National Park and Mount Desert Island Maine
with
FIELD GUIDE
and
ATLANTIS COMPARISON

J. Power Chaplin

To Shannon, Just because this book becomes valuable! June Chaplin

Hamilton, Edith and Cairns, Huntington; The Collected
Dialogues of Plato, Princeton UP, 1961, renewed 1989.
Reprinted by permission of Princeton University Press.

Dedicated
to the
Translators, Printers, and Librarians
who have made it possible for
us to ponder works that are
over 2000 year old

ISBN 0-9654411-0-5

©1996 J. Power Chaplin

Geoguide Publishing, Bar Harbor, Maine
Printed For Publisher by
Downeast Graphics & Printing
Ellsworth, Maine

An Expression of Appreciation
to
Don Eichler
Computer Consultant

THE NATIVE ROCK

The Celebrated Coastline

Acadia National Park and Mount Desert Island, Maine! What words describe adequately our celebrated coastline, the creation of our God?

The glorious skies! The blue of the north sky and the red and gold of sunset.

The moods of the ocean! The grace of its curling wave and the calm and brooding deep.

The carpeted forest! The rough and bristled pine tree and the soft and gentle fern.

And the bedrock underlying it all? Are the rocks described? The rugged rocks! They carry us to the heights of the mountains where we admire the forest and sea and sky. Our silent sentinels of time! Do we take the time to read their story of geologic past? This guide will help you to read the native rock.

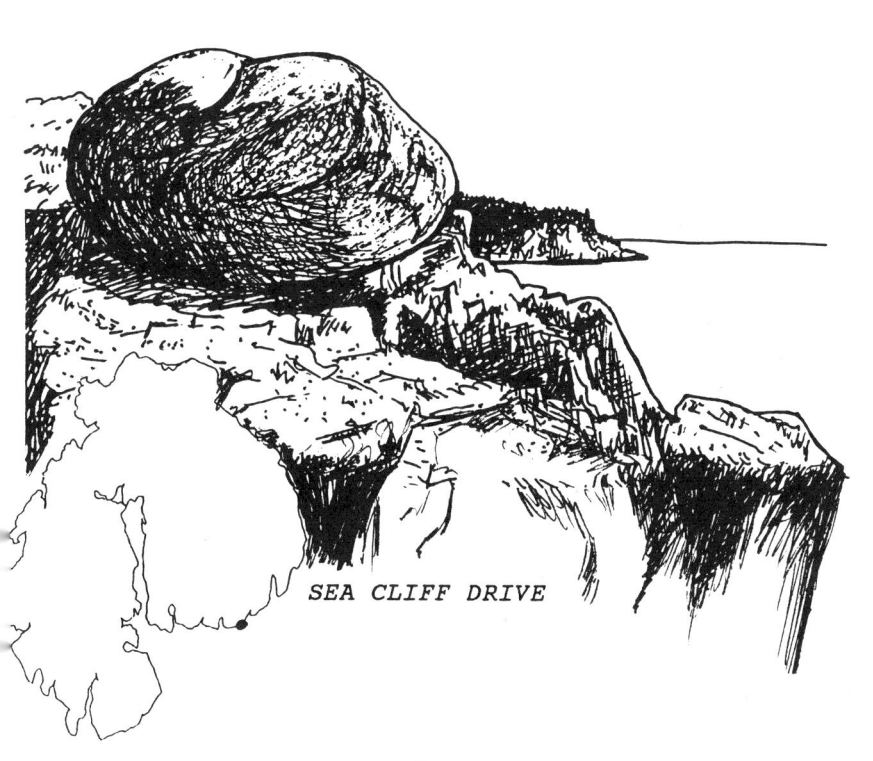

SEA CLIFF DRIVE

THE NATIVE ROCK

Background Information About the Earth

Earth is a big ball of rock. Simply put, it is a big ball in three layers: the crust, the mantle, and the core. The crust, of which the continents are made, extends from the surface to about 40 miles deep, and about 98% of it consists of only 8 elements: 47% oxygen, 28% silicon, 8% aluminum, 5% iron, 3% calcium, and over 2% each of sodium, potassium, and magnesium. All other elements found in the crust make up the remaining 2% (Silver and gold are so rare that they make up only .000,000,4% and .000,000,1 % of the crust.) These elements systematically combine in different ways to form a wide variety of minerals.

The heavier mantle, which underlies the continents and ocean basins, is made up predominantly of iron and magnesium. A drill has never reached the mantle, but it is believed that the molten rock there is a dark and heavy material called basalt.

The core of the earth consists of the heaviest elements, iron and nickel. Both the mantle and core are liquids; however, the word "molten" is better, for it implies a heavy, dense, slow-moving state. Both the mantle and core comprise the bulk of the earth. The thin crust, by comparison, is the "egg shell which contains the white of the egg and its heavy yolk."

Rocks are composed of one or more minerals. The types of igneous, sedimentary, and metamorphic define for us the origin of the mineral deposit. Igneous rocks are those that form within the earth in chambers called plutons. The mantle of the earth opens and molten rock called magma moves upward through the crust. When the molten rock reaches the surface, it forms volcanoes and lava flows, both extrusive features. Where it cools and solidifies below the surface, it forms plutons, sills, dikes and veins, all intrusive features.

IGNEOUS FORMATIONS

THE NATIVE ROCK

Sedimentary rock is made up of layers of sand, silt, clay, and mud, which are the products of surface erosion and redeposition. It consists of the eight common elements of the crust plus other elements found in smaller amounts. The layers accumulate on a sea floor where sediments wash from land and build thick layers often miles deep. The weight of the layers plus the weight of the sea water compresses the rock to make it solid. It does not acquire the strength and durability of igneous rock, however.

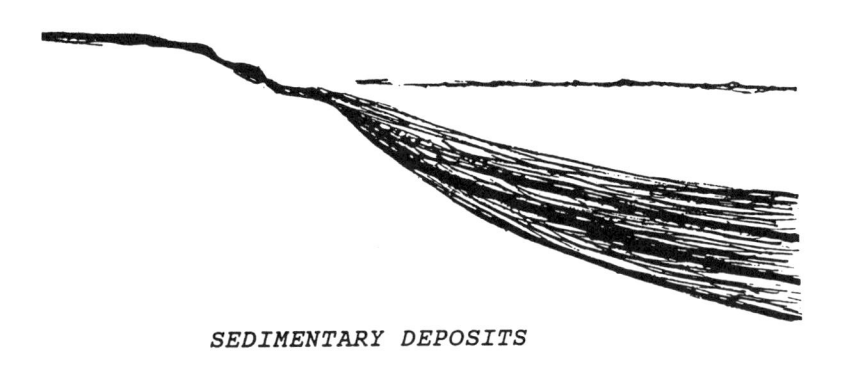

SEDIMENTARY DEPOSITS

Sedimentary rock forms on the land and in the sea also when layers of ash fall from volcanoes. The material is most often tuff or breccia.

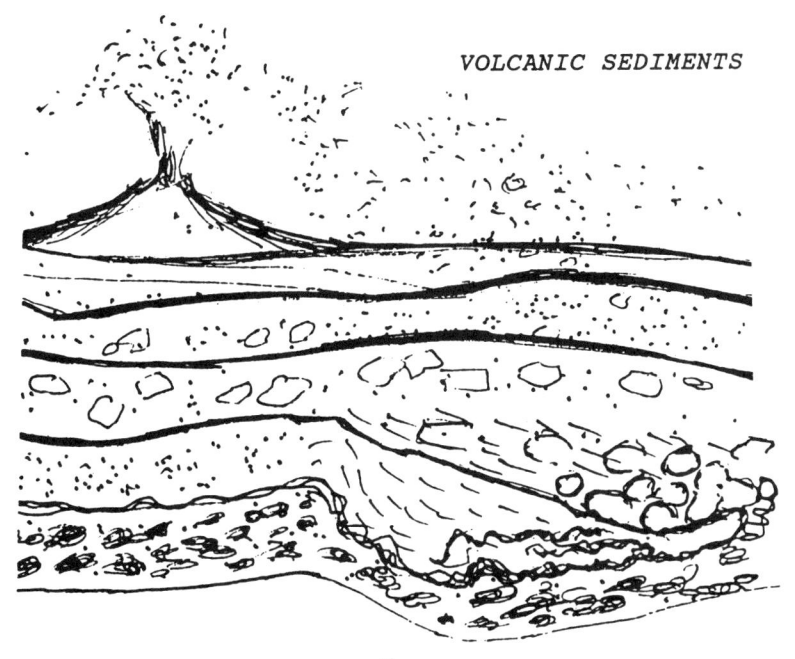

VOLCANIC SEDIMENTS

THE NATIVE ROCK

Metamorphic rock is altered rock, changed by heat and pressure. It is altered igneous and sedimentary rock that is changed by the heat and pressure of an underlying batholith or by the downfolding of the rock into the crust. To change rock, temperatures of 200-800 degrees are needed. (When rock of any type is changed by temperatures over 800 degrees for an extended period of time, the rock becomes igneous.) The altered rock shows folding and banding. Among the folds and bands emerge pods and irregular deposits of minerals as the elements regroup.

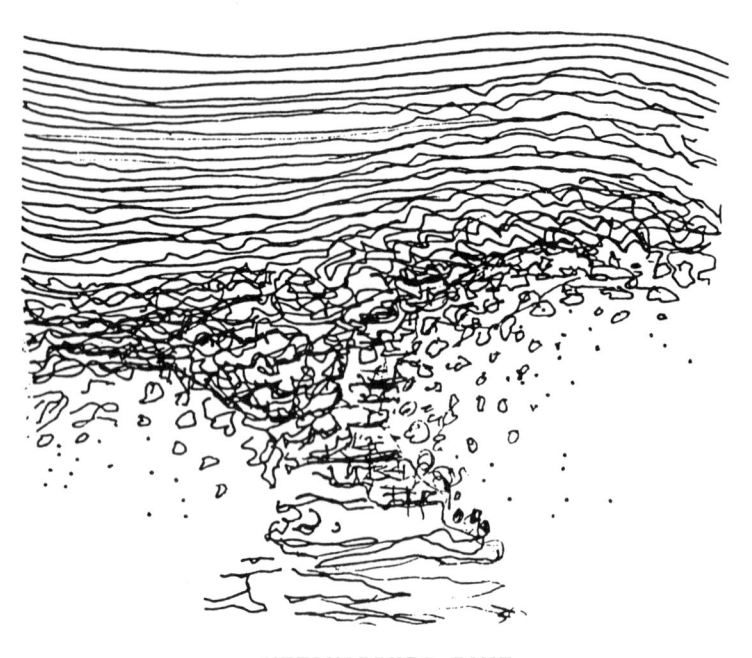

METAMORPHIC ZONE

THE NATIVE ROCK

The Identification of the Igneous Rock of Mount Desert Island

On Mount Desert Island, the igneous rock cooled within the crust under deep layers of sedimentary and metamorphic rocks, which were folded into a high mountain range, a part of the root system of the Appalachian Mountain Range. As time passed, the rocks were eroded away until the igneous rock was exposed. Today you will find more igneous rock in the bedrock surface underfoot, but remnant layers and broken stone of the other two types are easy to find.

There are two theories for magma intrusion that relate to the MDI area. In one, the MDI igneous rocks belong to separate plutons that lifted through the crust at different times. Each had a separate and different composition.

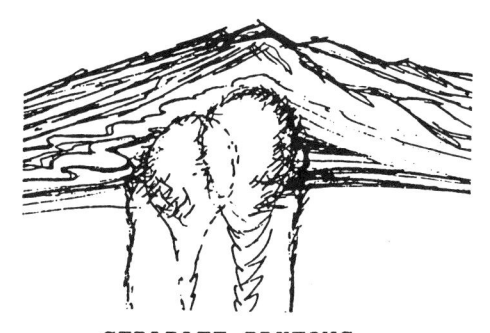

SEPARATE PLUTONS

In the other, one magma mass was influenced in different ways at different times which produced rock that shows a blending of composition across the land. In this guide the second theory is favored: The igneous rocks are seen originating from one source.

The igneous rocks are the youngest of the bedrock. They were formed between 50-380 million years ago. Two types, gabbro and diorite, are similar having come from the source first. They are grained rocks made up of two minerals, black pyroxene and white or gray feldspar. Gabbro has more dark minerals than light; diorite has more light than dark.

They formed great, horizontal sheets called sills many miles across when the mantle opened and a thick black basalt moved upward into the layers and folds of overlying sedimentary and metamorphic rock. Where the gabbro or diorite sills cooled more quickly, a fine grain was left, and where they cooled more slowly, a medium or coarse grain was left.

THE NATIVE ROCK

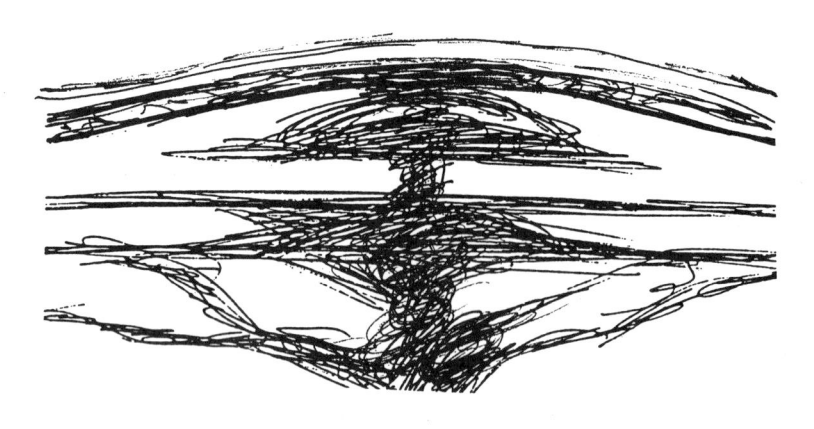

LACOLITHS & SILLS

The mountains of the island are made of granite, for after the gabbro-diorite sills had cooled, the magma mass became active again. Its composition changed. The igneous rock took on a third mineral, quartz. Together with dark and heavy minerals from the mantle and the lighter feldspar from the crust, quartz from the surface was melted into the magma to form granite. Because of the differences in the surface, the granite composition varies across the island, consequently, there are three major types.

GRANITE MAGMA ABOVE SILLS

At the time of their formation, the continents pushed against one another to form the one land mass called Pangea between 350-400 million years ago. The result was magma from the mantle pushed into the crust. Enough uplifted magma to form immense mountain ranges! During the struggle between the

THE NATIVE ROCK

continents, the main body of "MDI" granite, a small part of the uplifting material, burst deep within the earth. A large amount of this magma slumped out of the main chamber to form a thick deposit adjacent to it <u>deep within the earth</u>, and a large amount of the magma spread out to form granite sheets which were thinner and which cooled more quickly in geologic time. The main body and its thickly deposited prodigy cooled to have a coarse grain while the thinner masses that extruded from it cooled to fine and medium grains.

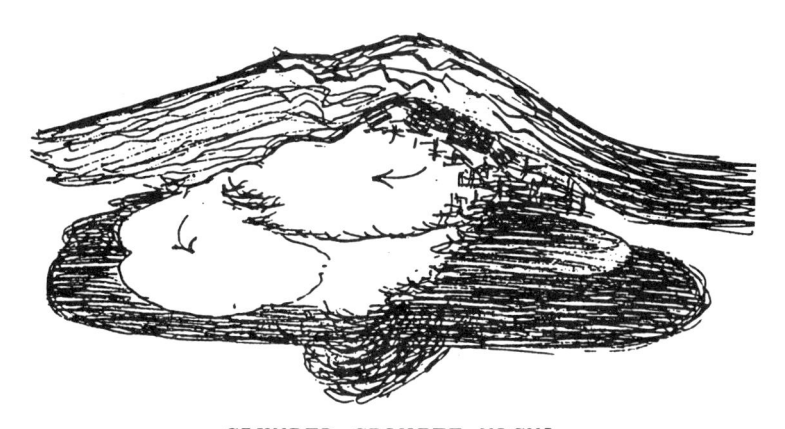

SLUMPED GRANITE MAGMA

The two forces that pushed the magma chamber were the two continents, Africa and Europe. During the folding of the land of the super continent of Pangea, the slumping magma carried shatter zone material with it. Areas within the main granite body have recrystallized rock which may indicate the pathways of the slumping magma as it poured through its own boundary to form neighboring granites.

Today we know the coarse grained rock as Cadillac granite and the fine to medium grained rocks as Southwest Harbor and Somesville granites. The mountains of the island are made up of Cadillac granite. On the eastern side of Somes Sound, there are mountains that belong to the main body, and on the western side, there are mountains of the prodigy, with thinner masses of the fine and medium grained granites to the north and south of the coarse grained.

Surrounding the main body of Cadillac granite, a zone of intermediate rock formed. Broken fragments were melted into the hot magma. This is known as a contact or shatter zone.

THE NATIVE ROCK

However, the story is not over. The slumped main body had an overlying ro(of?)
which we know melted into the granite. There were also blocks of the ro(ck?)
which fell into the chamber. The weight of the blocks may have caused th(e?)
cupolas that surround the granites. These smaller bubbles of pink grani(te?)
appear to be the tops of deeply lying granite. The special granites at Seawa(ll?)
and Bass Harbor are cupolas.

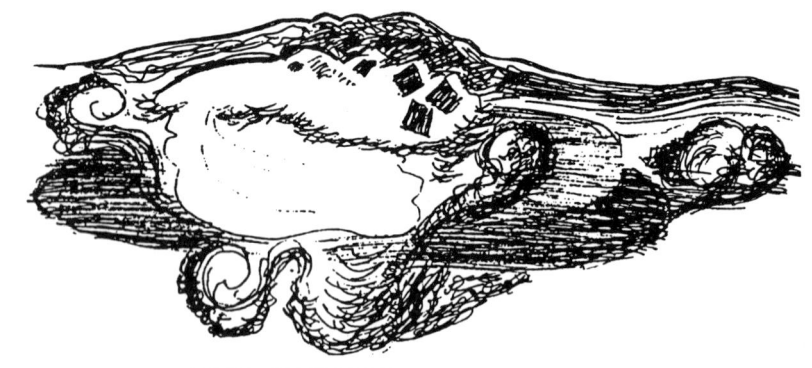

ROOF COLLAPSE & CUPOLA FORMATIONS

One unpopular theory explains that the main granite batholith may have blow(n?)
during some point in its molten life. This would account for the volcanics in th(e?)
area bedrock. However, geologists believe the volcanics of the Cranberry Islan(d?)
Series and Ovens to be the material of volcanoes to the southwest of Mou(nt?)
Desert Island.

UNPOPULAR THEORY

THE NATIVE ROCK

Of the granites on Mount Desert Island, the first to cool were the Southwest Harbor granites. They are fine to medium grained. They have an abundance of feldspar and quartz minerals with very small traces of the dark minerals, hornblende and biotite mica. The rock may appear light gray or tan.

The second to solidify were Somesville granites. They are fine to medium grained. They have gray feldspar and a pink feldspar, quartz, and black biotite mica.

The last to solidify and the largest quantity are the Cadillac granites. They are coarse grained. They have the dark mineral hornblende and some biotite mica, gray and translucent quartz, and a deep pink feldspar. The Cadillac granites make up the highest elevations of the island, the mountains of the island.

The names of Southwest Harbor, Somesville, and Cadillac were given to the granites for the places where they were found in the bedrock. The boundary lines between them blend, and deposits of one granite appear in another granite's territory.

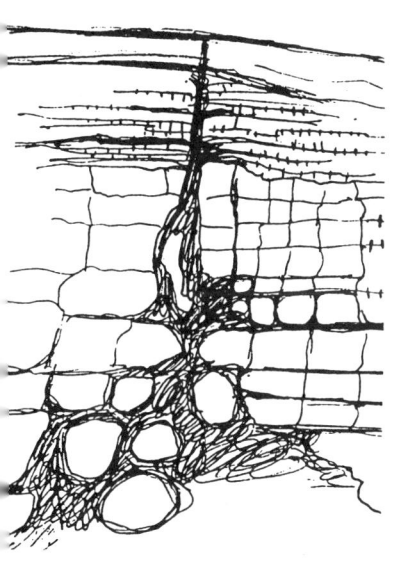

SHATTER ZONE   BOULDER OF THE SHATTER ZONE

The contact or shatter zone surrounding these granites also varies; for example, the zone along the western border of the island contains a granite/diorite matrix with fragments of Avalonian metamorphic while the zone along the northeastern border contains granite with Bar Harbor Series sedimentary rock.

THE NATIVE ROCK

The Formation of the Sedimentary Rock of Mount Desert Island

The sedimentary rocks of Mount Desert Island include two sets of materials, the Bar Harbor Series and the Cranberry Island Series. The names of the deposits were given for the locations where they were first studied. The Bar Harbor sediments were formed on a sea floor about 375 millions years ago. They are dense sandstones and softer siltstones that form layers of different thicknesses. The layers are commonly lavender and gray with some green and black, the latter colors where living and decayed matter were added. These layers rust when exposed to air, for they contain iron which oxidizes to form a reddish rust at the surface.

Three very unusual layers of the Bar Harbor Series can be seen at the Ovens, a seashore in Salisbury Cove which was named for small sea caverns that are also found there. Two black layers rich in carbon are separated by a wide green band containing chlorite. The carbon was derived from decayed matter and the chlorite from living plants, probably algae from an ancient sea. Above these three layers, there is a deposit of felsite and tuff which contains eroded, greenish concretions. Geologists believe the volcanic layers are not a part of the Cranberry Island Series although they are similar. Both the black sediments and unexplained concretions add to the mystery of the island's geologic history! The second sedimentary rock is called the Cranberry Island Series. Since there is a difference of opinion, an age is not given. Some of the volcanic sediments appear to have been compressed near the time of the Bar Harbor Series; some of it more recently. Perhaps the volcanics do not belong to one series but to several series of close but different ages. These layers were formed both on land and in the sea when volcanic material built up.

Four types of volcanic sediments can be found in the Cranberry Island Series. 1. They include tuff, a dense rock of fine ash which is gray or buff. With a hand lens, small spaces can be seen among the particles. The layers formed when ash fell from a volcano. 2. They include lava flows which are gray to black and which show flow marks and air spaces. These have been eroded in most locations. 3. There are areas of felsite which are reddish to yellowish brown where weathered at the surface and white, light gray and yellow at a fresh cut. Felsite is a material of feldspar and silica, which if left to cool slowly over a long time within the earth, would form a granite. Both lava flows and felsites are of igneous origin but cooled in layers with ash and sediments to form layers of sedimentary rock. 4. There are breccias of large and broken rocks of the crust cemented within fine ash.

THE NATIVE ROCK

A Description of the Metamorphic Rock of Mount Desert Island

The metamorphic rock on Mount Desert Island was called, locally, the Bartlett Island Series and the Ellsworth Schist. More recently, it was identified as the rock of the Avalon Peninsula in Newfoundland. The Avalonian metamorphic rock is over 500 million years old and is the bedrock of a narrow zone found in Connecticut, Rhode Island, Massachusetts, Eastern Maine, New Brunswick, and Newfoundland in North America and in small areas of Southern Ireland, Wales, and Central England in Europe. It is theorized that a continent of Avalonian rock once existed, only remnants of which are found today.

The Avalonian metamorphic rock was once sedimentary layers of mud and silt in an ancient sea. They are rich in chlorite, the green color of living matter. They contain the fossil of the paradoxides trilobite. The layers were deposited in an ancient sea and metamorphosed by heat and pressure. Other colors include the white opaque quartz of the pods and irregular accumulations and the silvery gray of its quartz schist or mica. Within its deposit, there is gneiss which are like schists but which show less folding and more striations.

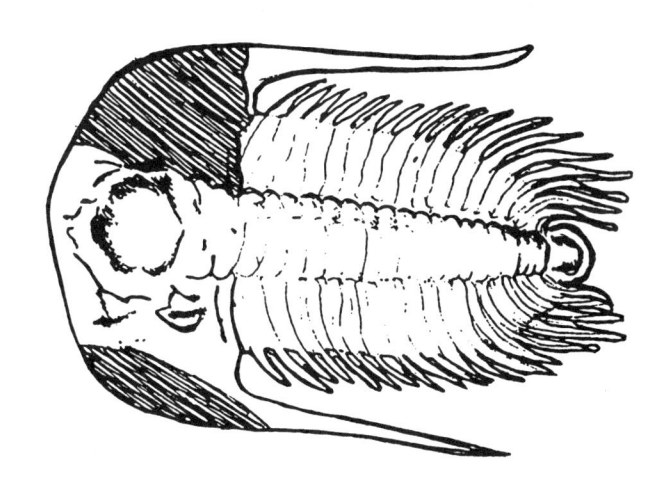

PARADOXIDES TRILOBITE

Good locations to examine bedrock types: To find the rocks, check the bedrock map and drive to locations where roadcuts may be examined. Search for fresh

THE NATIVE ROCK

cuts along the blasted surfaces of roadcuts, and please do not make any cut yourself to expose fresh rock. Be forewarned, for the rock at the surface will be stained by weathering, decayed vegetation, and the growth of lichens.

Visiting one of the beaches on the southern border of the island is a better idea. Here you will find all the rock types because the glacier of under 13,000 years ago lifted and carried broken rocks from the north to the south. Look for rocks that are washed clean by the ocean waves.

On all the beaches of Mount Desert Island, you will find a rock not from the island bedrock. The glacier, as it flowed NW-SE, carried a coarse grained white granite called Lucerne granite to the island. Many of the large erratics, rocks carried by the glacier, like Balance Rock in Bar Harbor and Bubble Rock on South Bubble Mountain in Acadia National Park are Lucerne granite. The rock is the bedrock of Lucerne, Maine, about 40 miles to the northwest. This granite is easy to spot for the rectangular feldspar grains are very large, up to an inch across.

Other erratics that you will find are the broken pieces of basalt and diabase taken from dikes and stones of quartz from veins that cut through the island. Dikes and veins were formed deep within the earth. They are mineral deposits that filled weak zones, cracks, and fractures within the magma as it cooled and contracted and as the continental plates rifted apart.

The word "diabase" refers to a number of different compositions of basalt material in which lighter minerals were added. It is not as heavy and black as basalt, but it is rich in magnesium and iron. Diabase is black, dark gray, and gray. The word is used often in this guide, and it covers a number of dark rocks.

Three good locations for the exploration of rock types are suggested. They are close to the highways. Although walking is for short distances, good shoes are needed for occasional climbs over boulders.

Check the tides before setting out. You need not wait for low tide, however. An hour or two before or after high tide will give you enough room at the top of the beach where you will find cobblestones to examine.

The three beaches include Bracy's Cove and adjacent shoreline in Seal Harbor; Seawall, south of Southwest Harbor in Acadia National Park; and the Causeway, south of Bar Harbor, in Acadia National Park on the Park Loop Road.

THE NATIVE ROCK

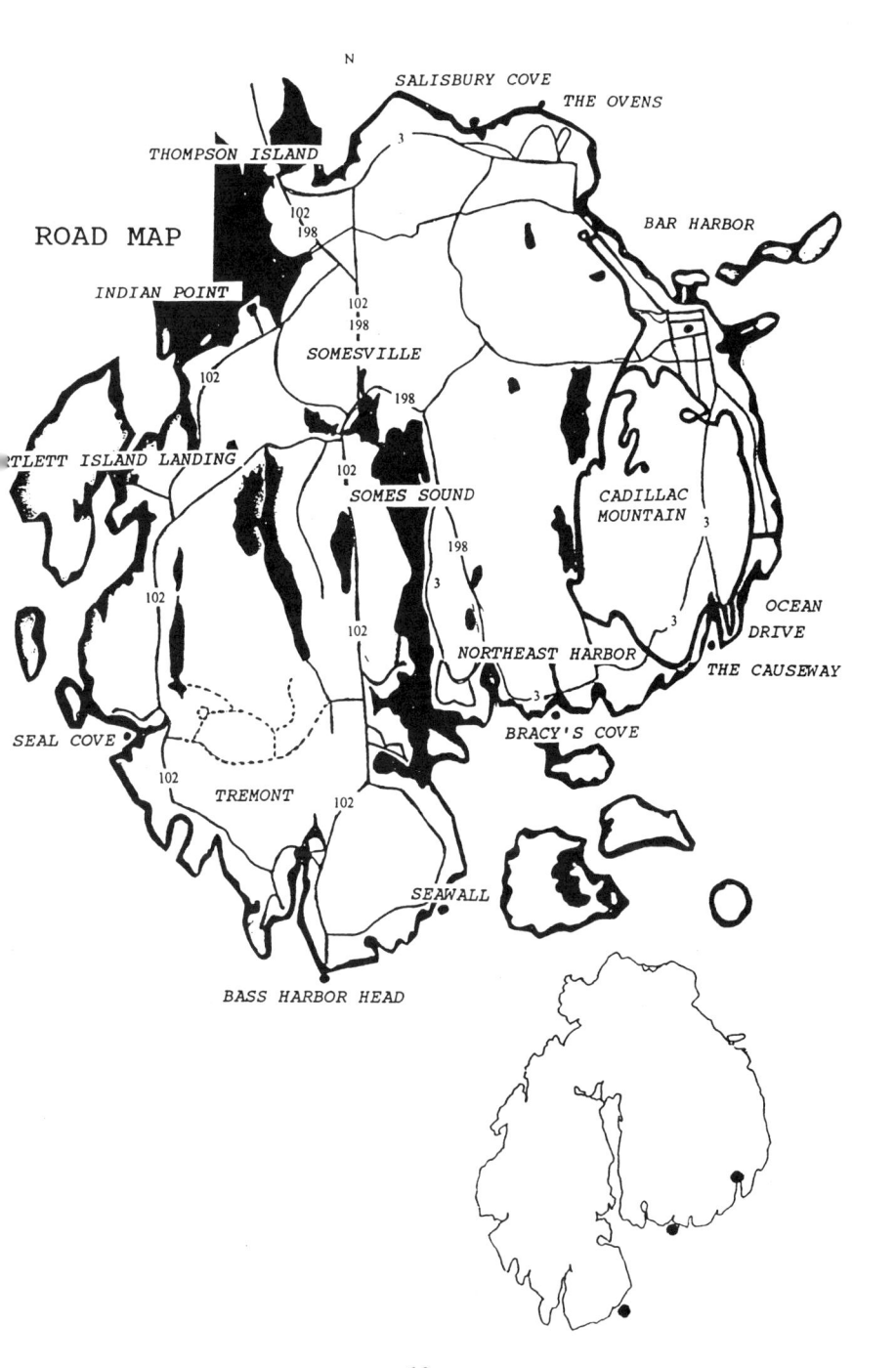

ROAD MAP

THE NATIVE ROCK

AFTER GEOLOGICAL SURVEY MAP, 1956

BEDROCK MAP

✣ CUPOLA GRANITE

- AVALONIAN METAMORPHIC
- BAR HARBOR SERIES
- DIORITE
- CRANBERRY ISLAND SERIES, FELSITE
- CRANBERRY ISLAND SERIES, TUFF AND BRECCIA
- GRANITE
- SHATTER ZONE

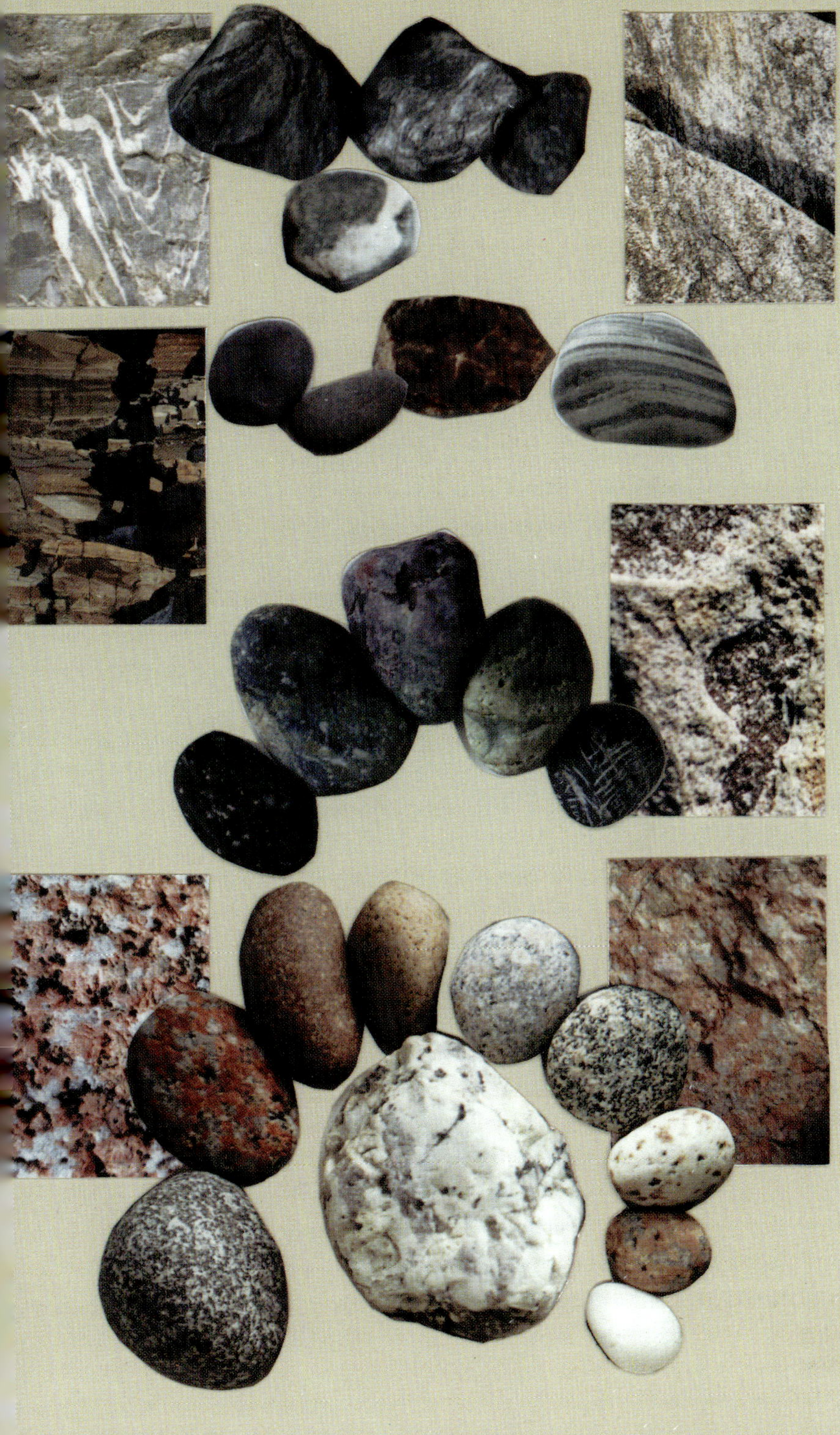

ROCKS OF MOUNT DESERT ISLAND

Top Row: AVALONIAN METAMORPHIC
    1. schist bedrock
    2. four schist pebbles
    3. gneiss bedrock

Second Set: BAR HARBOR SERIES SEDIMENTS
    4. sandstone and siltstone layers
    5. two sandstone pebbles
    6. felsite
    7. quartzite (metamorphic)

Third Set: CRANBERRY ISLAND SERIES
    8. lava flow pebble
    9. four breccia pebbles
    10. tuff bedrock

Fourth Collection: MDI's IGNEOUS ROCKS
    11. Cadillac granite bedrock
    12. diorite cobble
    13. Cadillac granite pebble
    14. felsite
    15. Southwest Harbor granite pebble
    16. two Somesville granite pebbles
    17. two cupola granites
    18. quartz pebble
    19. Somesville's granite at the Whaleback and Patty Lot Hill
    20. Lucerne granite cobble (adopted)

THE NATIVE ROCK

Rifts and Drifts

A Global Explanation of Mount Desert Island Bedrock

The rocks that you see at Mount Desert Island are located today at 44 degrees North Latitude, but they were not formed that far north. The land mass of Avalonia has been on the move for over 400 million years. The Avalonian land mass may have been a continent or may have been a part of northwestern Africa. It was put down as layers of mud and silt in an ancient sea far south of the equator over 500 million years ago. They were metamorphosed later, perhaps "en route." Just as the other land areas began to move from the southern hemisphere into the northern, Avalonia drifted slowly until it collided with the continent of North America about 350-400 million years ago. During the welding years, the Bar Harbor and Cranberry Island Series were compressed.

During this phase also, the igneous rocks of our island were solidified about 360-380 million years ago well below the surface. Since they cooled after the sedimentary rocks were compressed, they are considered younger. The mantle provided the dark material of the magma while the crustal rocks that belonged to the land mass provided the light minerals, and at this time the continents were passing the equator. At this time the continents had pushed into each other and had formed the Appalachians in North America, the Caledonians in Europe, and the Atlas Mountains in Africa. The name Pangea is given to the land mass that extended from the North to South Poles while a vast ocean occupied the other half of the globe.

At about 225 million years ago, the whole land mass started breaking apart. The first separation came between Africa and Europe, forming an early ocean gulf, which rifted apart until it had sliced to North America; then the separation changed direction and Africa was sliced from America. Some of Africa was left behind in North America and some of North America was left behind in Africa. During this phase, the continents had drifted more northward. The Avalonian bedrock (along with its acquired sedimentary and igneous deposits) developed large cracks in the crust as North America and Africa pulled away from each other. The cracks were filled with dark diabase minerals from the mantle above the equator. They became our northeasterly dikes which can be found in all the rock types on the island except the Cadillac granites.

Note: Dike formation may have preceded ocean rifting by 100 million years, it being possibly a transition phase between continental collision or orogeny and continental separation.

THE NATIVE ROCK

DIKE FORMATION

About 200 million years ago, Europe began to separate from the northeastern United States and Canada. The continents were pulled apart, and a second set of cracks were formed as the land stretched. More hot magma filled the cracks, and our island was stitched up a second time. These formed the second set of dikes that run in a northwesterly direction on the island which can be found in all rock types including the Cadillac granites.

And the Avalonian bedrock was also split up. Some of it remained in the northeastern United States and Canada and some was to become bedrock of the British Isles.

The idea of Continental Drift was old when Alfred Wegener first considered it. However, he gathered evidence that the continents of Africa and South America were once joined. He compared their similar biologies, bedrock geologies, and climates. He spoke of "Pangaea" in 1912 and in 1924 he wrote <u>The Origins of the Continents and Oceans</u>.

However, it was not until 1960 that the drifting of continents was explained. Scientists provided the idea of seafloor spreading from mid-oceanic ridges that were being mapped by sonar for the first time. The ocean floors rift from the ridges. Continents drift because oceans rift.

THE NATIVE ROCK

TWO DIKES AT SCHOODIC POINT

Rifts are openings through which upwelling magma lifts and falls to each side. The rift zones lie dormant for thousands of years; then they open as basalt lifts and spreads. The ocean floors have been drilled for bedrock samples. The rock of the ocean floor is basalt.

The ocean floors have been measured for magnetic alignment. On each side of a rift, there are bands of rock magnetized in a North to South direction showing that the iron particles within the rock were influenced by the earth's magnetic field. These bands are adjacent to older bands that show a reversal. The ocean floor of basalt has an irregular alternating pattern of magnetic alignment.

Within the molten rock are iron elements that are influenced by the earth's magnetic field. The earth, itself, is a giant magnet and the pull of the North Pole attracts the particles to align in a North to South direction. To the east and west of the Mid-Atlantic Rift, bands of rock show alternating magnetism, N-S and S-N.

One theory proposes that the earth's magnetic field reverses, that the North Pole reverses to the South Pole while the South becomes the North every million years or so.

THE NATIVE ROCK

A second theory explains that a S-N zone was determined by a N-S zone to balance the electromagnetic field of the more immediate area. When the internal struggle balances, the earth's electromagnetic field again influences the ocean floor for a N-S alignment. The N-S or positive charge continues to grow stronger until the ocean floor no longer responds to polar control but to the internal N-S or positive charge of neighboring rock and reverses to S-N or negative charge.

To understand the first theory, think of the iron particles within the molten rock like compass points which will point to North. The tiny iron particles move in the molten rock to show that direction.

To understand the second theory, think of small bar magnets lined up on a tabletop. They are too heavy to move themselves as the lighter compass point, but they are so strongly influenced by what lies next to them, that two magnets both pointing N-S will repel each other, end to end and side by side as well. Two magnets of opposite magnetism, one N-S and the other S-N, strongly attract one another. They make a strong bond. The iron particles in molten rock, unlike the heavy bar magnets on a tabletop, can align N-S or reverse S-N.

The sea floor spreads an average of 1 cm a year; however, a rift zone may rest for thousands of years, then open. The rifting over the last 200 million years has been slow at times and violently active at other times. The opening is rarely wider than a meter. Eruptions of magma have been filmed. Magma so hot that it glows yellow and red rolls to the top of the rift. There is an intriguing center line of flow that seems to hesitate before magma pours over the opening and down both sides. The hesitancy is followed by sudden rises to one side, then to the other. After it rolls to the side, it soon cools and becomes black basalt rock. Once hardened, the iron particles are trapped in position. Lava flows show reversals also. One layer above another may align and reverse. Both theories explain this difference of magnetic reversal equally well.

Many of the dikes on Mount Desert Island show a center fill line just as rifts do. The magma that lifted through them may also have flowed or poured upward in a similar way. Within the Cadillac granite mountains, there are pink dikes of felsite which may be fill lines as well. Think of your toothpaste tube. When you squeeze it, the paste flows or pours through the tube through the center and leaves behind within the tube, a space that will fill with paste the next time you squeeze it. Felsite is a material which would have formed a grained granite if it had been given more time; however, when the felsic magma stopped along its course way, it cooled quickly.

THE NATIVE ROCK

Although ocean floors spread, the globe does not become a larger sphere because the continents subduct as they are pushed against one another. There are 16 major plates: some are made up of the continental bedrock of igneous, sedimentary and metamorphic rock, and some are the oceanic plates of basalt. Along the collision lines are subduction zones or trenches. The heavier oceanic plates dip down under the lighter continents.

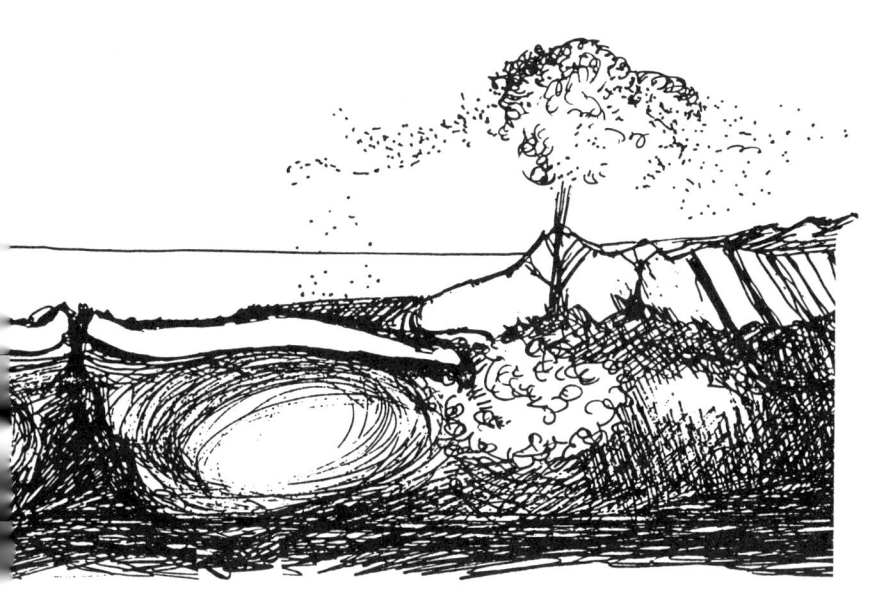

OROGENY

These zones are called zones of orogeny. As basalt is subducted along with ocean sediments that have accumulated on them, the mantle becomes active and hot and sends up plutons of molten material. Volcanoes and lava flows form. This happened along the Northeast when the continents pushed one another, and in the area of Mount Desert Island, the Mount Desert Range was formed.

The range uplifted when a magma chamber folded up layers of Avalonian metamorphic and acquired sedimentary deposits between 360-380 million years ago. Later, when the continents broke up between 225-200 million years ago, sets of northeasterly and northwesterly dikes were formed when hot magma filled cracks left by the plates which stretched apart. In the United States, Canada, Greenland, and Europe, there are trending dikes that radiate toward the Mid-Atlantic.

THE NATIVE ROCK

No one knows the reason for the rifting that pushes the land masses. It has been suggested that a body must have left the earth, perhaps the moon, and that rifting and drifting help to balance the weight loss. It has been suggested that a body hit the earth, an asteroid from space, that started the disturbance within the earth. It has been proposed that the tidal waters that bulge over the mid-oceanic rifts push the oceanic plates into the crust. Perhaps it has something to do with the earth's rotation and the gravitational attraction of other bodies in the solar system. Perhaps the earth's crust is upset by the Ice Ages that come and go in cycles alternating with Warm Ages. Most geologists believe the earth's center core and mantle are cooling which results in convection currents within the mantle which causes the rifting and drifting. The fascinating ideas add to the mystery!

MOUNTAIN BUILDING OROGENY

THE NATIVE ROCK

Planes Aflame

A Description of the Quartz Veins

The outside of a magma chamber cools before its interior. Hot magma is left within the center which does not cool for a long time. It is heated by the mantle below it, for the molten rock is deep within the earth.

As the magma of the Cadillac granites cooled, the stone contracted. Fractures developed in the hardened rock. Fault lines resulted where the fractures were long. Running northwesterly, there is an outcropping of quartz on the island. It seems to follow a fault line in the granite bedrock from Sea Cliff Drive in Seal Harbor toward Seal Harbor Beach. It can be seen in several locations continuing on in its northwest direction to Northeast Harbor. It is about three feet wide at Sea Cliff Drive, but in higher elevations it separates into several ribbons, one to two inches wide.

As cracks appeared overhead in the hardened granite, minerals and water from the surface of the earth leaked down into the vat. The cracks varied in size, some large openings and others tapered to veins the thinness of threads. The openings were not cylindrical like the veins of the body, however. The openings were broad planes more like wide and thin ribbons that opened and filled possibly over 10,000 feet deep.

Over time, the minerals within the molten center of the magma chamber were attracted to each other to form three different molten masses. The quartz solution bubbled and boiled within the deep chamber. The hot syrup became explosive, but it was not the first to solidify or crystallize.

The molten feldspar sloshed and stewed. It would intrude and fill cracks also, but the medium weight feldspar would not be the first to vacate the magma chamber either.

The heavy diabase near the bottom of the chamber rolled and groaned. It would be the first to solidify. To remain molten, it required the highest temperatures of the three minerals. It came from deeper in the mantle where the temperatures were great. Since it was cooler at the surface, it was the first to harden. Think of the tube of toothpaste again. It was squeezed. The more volatile solutions slid around, probably flying everywhere and hardening nowhere, while the thick material was pushed out of the tube. It filled the first cracks that appeared.

THE NATIVE ROCK

The feldspar filled cracks, finer fractures for the most part, that appeared later as the chamber continued to cool, and the hot and fluid quartz filled the finest and most intricate network of weak zones that resulted nearer the surface. The quartz was the last mineral to crystallize in the earth.

Since the internal cooling of the MDI granite masses coincided with the breaking up of the super continent Pangea, the stretching crust intensified dike development. Our basalt and diabase dikes were both influenced by and helped with the rifting and drifting mechanism at work in the mid-Atlantic today. This seems to be how the earth is healed, for the process of continental drift continually alters the crust.

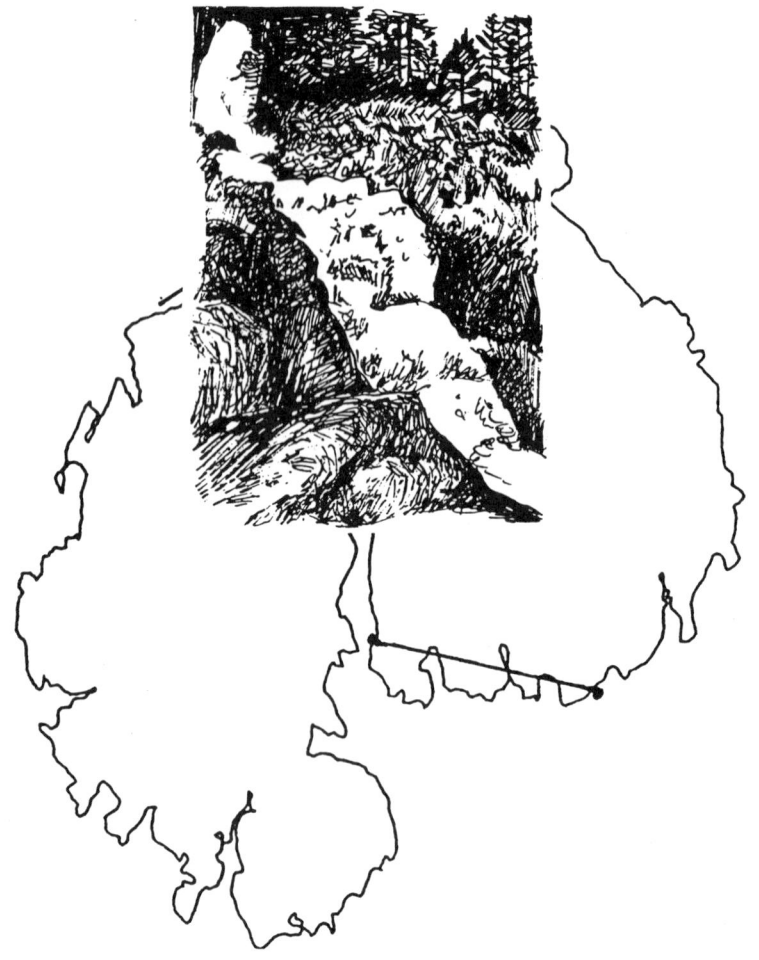

QUARTZ & DIABASE IN FAULTLINE

THE NATIVE ROCK

The Quarried Rock

The Story of Glacial Carving

Approximately 2-3 million years ago, the earth cooled. Snow fell at the two poles which built up into thick ice sheets. It is not known if the continental sheets built quickly or slowly in geologic time. An Ice Age began. It was not the first. Evidence shows that Ice Ages have existed between interglacial Warm Ages.

It is believed that the last ice sheet called the Wisconsin formed under 2 million years ago. The full impact of the Wisconsin Ice Sheet came about 20,000 years ago and began to recede between 13,000 and 14,000 years ago in the Mount Desert Island area. During that time glacial ice in thicknesses of over one mile covered the northern hemisphere from the North Pole to 40 degrees North Latitude. In the southern hemisphere, ice reached from the South Pole to 60 degrees South Latitude.

The mountain ranges of the world were covered with thick alpine glaciers that connected one another and which projected canyon glaciers down their flanks.

Before the glacier receded, the oceans held less water for great amounts of water were trapped in ice. The oceans were saltier, denser, colder, and slower. The ocean to the southwest of Mount Desert Island was offshore, more than 300 miles, while glacial ice moved over land that one day would become the continental shelf. The great weight of the ice depressed the earth crust into the mantle. It is believed that 3000 feet of ice can depress the crust 1000 feet.

The North Atlantic was covered with solid pack ice in the north connecting Maine, Nova Scotia, Newfoundland, Greenland, Iceland, the British Isles, and Scandinavia. The ocean to the south carried ice flows and icebergs that drifted slowly about the heavy sea. The ocean water in the North Atlantic over 14,000 years ago was not the water we know today.

The climate to the north was cold and dry. The climate near the equator was hot and dry. The sky was bright and blue with cloud cover uncommon. Near the equator, melted water from glacial ice entered the salty sea and formed shallow inland seas. How could the lower latitudes be so hot and dry with so much ice and water to the north and south of them? As the weight of the ice pushed the crust of the earth down, the mantle may have bulged upward into the crust of the equatorial regions and any other area without heavy ice. That would have brought the hot magma close to the surface. As the ice masses

THE NATIVE ROCK

advanced and receded during cooling and warming phases within the Ice Age, water flowed toward the lower latitudes, but the land there remained warm and dry with evaporation at the surface. Water that flowed underground formed hot springs and geysers. Underground water did not escape through evaporation so readily.

Water abounded under the deserts near the equator, and where it was drawn to the surface as geysers and natural springs, green spaces were created. Is it any wonder that early civilizations overpopulated the limited green areas? In winter snow fell over the glacier and rain fell over the deserts. In summer the ice melted and water evaporated. The cold and white ice to the north reflected the sun's rays and the earth remained cold except for the arid lower latitudes. After ice receded from the MDI area, magma near the surface may have given this area a warm climate.

If the oceans should shrink in the future, there would be great explorations on the continental shelf. Archaeologists believe they may have been occupied by early people after the glacier receded.

Living at the melting front of a glacier would have its advantages. Big game animals like the mammoths roamed the ice margins. There would be fresh water if a way could be found to filter it from the clay minerals it contained. There would be stratified deposits of sand and stone for construction purposes. If stone walls were built to retain soil deposits, there could be agriculture. Higher mounds called moraines would provide dry land as the glacier receded. If drainage ditches were built around them, they could be protected from the rivers and streams that flowed out of the glacier. Valuable minerals, especially metals, could be found in the freshly exposed rock. Large boulders being carried by the ice could have been lowered by ropes onto the outwash plain before the glacier to line wells or to make a protective wall or to build a house. This is probably what was done in the British Isles. Stonehenge may be the core structure of a building or well made from erratics which were lowered into place by people who knew how to live in front of the melting glacier.

Between 13,000 and 14,000 years ago, the ice began to melt in this area. This ended episodes of glacial carving that had gone on for at least 10,000 years. For a long time the ocean water took over the depression left behind by the melted ice, and a bigger ocean covered eastern Maine. The shoreline at that time was miles inland. An ocean existed over the lower elevations of Mount Desert Island to a depth of at least 210 feet. With the passage of time, the land rebounded. Today, beach heads and marine deposits can be found on the island's mountain slopes. It must have taken hundreds of years before the land

THE NATIVE ROCK

GLACIAL RECESSION

egan slowly to rebound to the position that we know today. The weight of the
eep ice sheets must have been far greater than that of the ocean that took its
lace, for the earth's crust lifted out of the mantle.

nly arctic varieties of sea life lived in this area for many years. Pulverized
ck from the base of the ice left by glacial rivers contain shell that dates to
2,250 years old. At that time a buildup of marine clay entrapped shells that
e found today in arctic regions. Since the shells are whole and in good shape,
e deposition was made in quiet water; however, there are deposits on MDI
at were made by violent water. These other deposits are steeply inclined and
dded with gravels and sands and boulders.

time the oceans filled with fresh water from glacial ice. The water absorbed
e sun's rays instead of reflecting them. The earth became warmer. Water
om the warmer oceans evaporated. Cloud cover, blown by air currents, caused
mospheric conditions not known previously. The surface ocean waters
came lighter, more fluid, and more powerful. The ocean became unsafe for
nall boats far at sea.

THE NATIVE ROCK

Glacial ice is still melting. The earth is still growing warmer. Occasional periods of cold bring temporary cold spells, but the earth grows warmer. Geologists record recently-exposed bedrock where mountain and arctic glaciers have melted. Oceanographers measure the rising sea level. Biologists note the changes in plant and animal life over the face of the earth.

The glacier left U-shaped valleys behind. As the massive glacier flowed over the island, it sought the weak zones of the rock and plowed it away. The remnant deposits of sedimentary and metamorphic rock were protected from the flowing ice by the more resistant granite batholiths which slowed the ice sheet so it could not carve as well.

The U-shaped valleys were carved between zones of more resistant rock. The side walls were left so steeply cut that talus deposits resulted in later years as blocks of granite fell beneath the cliffs. The blocks of talus have sharp and angular lines and surfaces unlike those rounded by the glacier or those ground by ocean waves. At the Tarn between Champlain and Dorr Mountains, there is a trail along the west side of the pond that crosses a talus deposit. The U-shaped valley between Pemetic Mountain and Cadillac contains the glacially-carved basin for Bubble Pond. Here you will see that the shallow lake is filled with glacial till.

THE TARN

THE NATIVE ROCK

Glacial polish and striations can be seen on many rock surfaces on Mount Desert Island. It is believed that the polish was once so perfect as to mirror images, but it has become dull over time. Still the polished rock reflects sunlight very well. In some areas, the rock is so smooth that climbing on it is difficult. At the Tarn on the east side of the highway at the pond's north end, a large bluff has been exposed in recent time that has good polish. For years the polished area was protected by till that covered it. When the highway was built and later widened, the till fell away to expose the polished stone. Now that it is exposed to the weather, it will in time become dull.

Glacial scratches and chatter marks are two more features formed by the abrasion of the ice. The scratches were formed by rock being dragged over rock under the heavy ice. The chatter marks are cusp-shaped cracks where the bedrock was scrubbed. Scrubbing granite required the weight of thick, heavy ice that froze only partially to the rock's surface. When the ice moved ahead, only small cusps of rock were torn from the bedrock. Most of the rock remained in place because a thin layer of rock flour or clay minerals between the ice and rock sanded rather than quarried the rock.

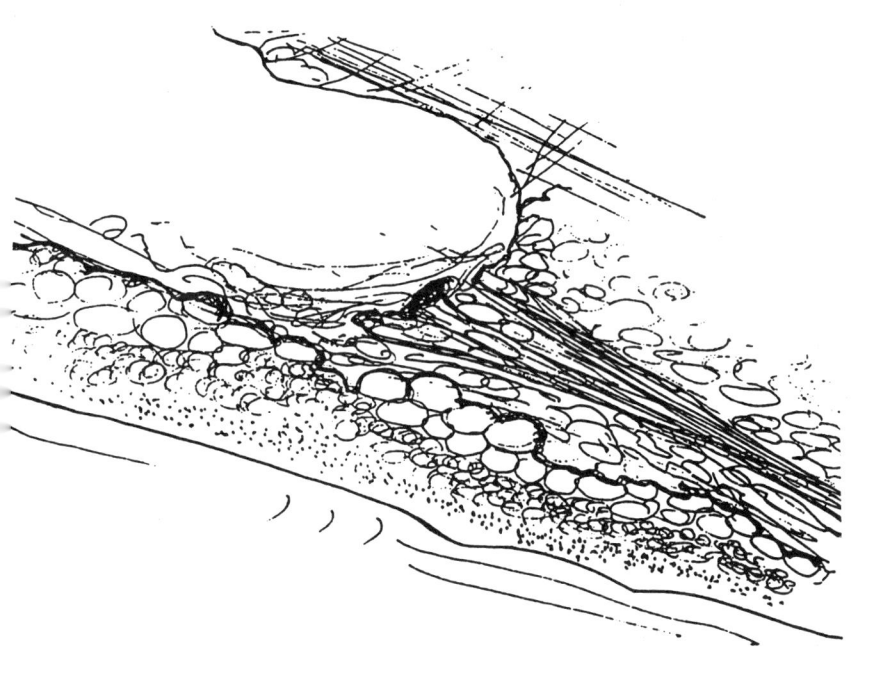

GLACIAL FEATURES

THE NATIVE ROCK

CHATTER MARKS *SURFACE CRACKS*

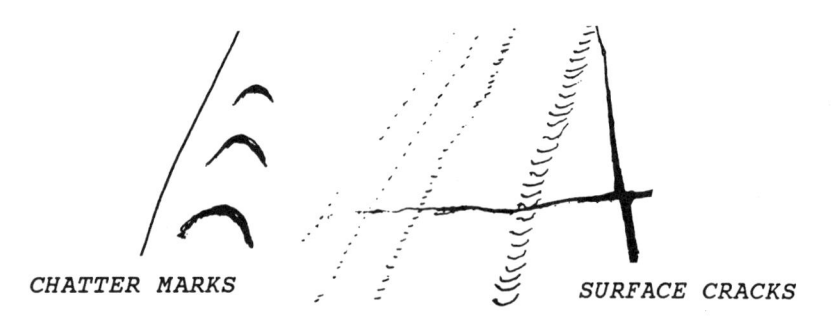

GLACIAL SCRATCHES

Erratics are stones moved by the glacier from one bedrock to another. On the island there are many boulders out of place. A coarse grained white granite from Lucerne, 40 miles northwest, has been scattered all over the island. Avalonian metamorphic rock and Cadillac granite also rest on bedrock of other rock types. The better known examples are both Lucerne granite: Balance Rock on the Shore Path in Bar Harbor and Bubble Rock on South Bubble in Acadia. However, there are many other large boulders to find. If you have learned the rock types, you will know an erratic when you see one. Just compare the rock to the bedrock it rests upon.

BUBBLE ROCK

THE NATIVE ROCK

Glacial ice was filled with dirt and stone. Its layers were clearly defined by the material within it. When it moved, the stone at its bottom surfaces acted as an abrasive on the bedrock that it was flowing over. When it melted, the debris dropped out.

Till is a deposit of unstratified debris, dropped out in deep piles whenever the ice slowed and melted. The rivers that flowed on, within, and under the glacier sorted the till by the size and weight of its material in stratified deposits.

TILL WITH ERRATICS

Clay deposits are stratified deposits. Clay minerals are accumulations of rock flour, fine mineral particles, transported by the glacial rivers and deposited in the sea. Clay minerals were taken from the feldspar in granite, worn away from bedrock by glacial ice over many years. Deposits of clay are found in coves and stream beds. Some were laid in quiet waters; others were deposited in steeply inclined beds by violent waters. This clay, which bakes to a red color, was used by the Abnaki Indian tribes for pottery.

On the island there are deposits of gravel and sand. However, just north of the island on the mainland, there are thick deposits in Lamoine which are used in construction. The beds of fine sand show layering from more than one melting; in fact, the area just north of the island is a flat outwash plain where the glacial sheet may have been slowed as it tried to push through the granite mountains of the island. It was slowed and stopped repeatedly in long enough pauses to allow layers of sand to melt out of the ice.

THE NATIVE ROCK

Before the Ice Age, the granite batholiths were eroded to a broad, peneplain that remained very high over the surrounding terrain. It may have been covered with worn sedimentary and metamorphic layers in many places, especially to the north of the east-west running ridge, and to the south. As the ice approached, its first advances tore into the weak joints and zones of the granite. It also took advantage of the N-S running diabase dikes. The mountains and lake basins show not only the direction of the moving ice, but also they show the weak interior zones of the granite. The more resistant granite mountains have a glacial shape called roches moutonnees or whaleback, for like a whale's back, the north slopes are gradual and smooth and the south slopes are steep. This shape can be seen in small ledges along the coast as well as in the mountains. After the glacier was finished with its carving, the island was left with the following major mountains: St. Sauveur, 679; Acadia, 681; Beech, 839; Norumbega, 852; Parkman, 941; Mansell, 949; Champlain, 1058; Bernard, 1071; Penobscot, 1194; Pemetic, 1248; Dorr, 1270; Sargent, 1373; and Cadillac, 1530 feet.

ISLAND ELEVATIONS

THE NATIVE ROCK

These mountains show the "loving hands" of glacial carving. The smooth surfaces are sometimes referred to as "P" formations, because the cutting is not only on the top surface but on under surfaces of rock as well. The ice hands held and gripped the rock so tightly that the rock was smoothed "lovingly" on many surfaces at once. There are cracks in many places that show that the rock could not have taken much more "caressing" without being quarried. Between the ice hands and the rock that was polished, there was a layer of rock flour that acted like fine sand paper. Without the rock flour, the ice would have frozen to the surface and plucking or quarrying would have resulted.

Because the island borders the sea today, it is easy to forget that in glacial time the Wisconsin Ice Sheet did not stop here but continued moving southeast another 300 miles to the edge of the Continental Shelf. Glacial features were formed under the ice as it advanced southeast. This area is under an ocean today.

AVALONIAN ERRATIC

THE NATIVE ROCK

The Rugged Coastline

An Exploration of Seashore Erosion

Approximately 3 million visitors are drawn to Acadia National Park's shoreline every year. Within the park and within the boundaries of the four Maine towns on Mount Desert Island, there are miles of coastline to explore. The high headlands, the rugged ledges, the wave-worn beaches, sandy bars and mud flats await you.

The beaches are young landform features by geologic time. Eroded by ocean waves since the receding of the glacier, the coastline offers the pleasant composition of sky, sea, forest and rock.

The ocean waves are created by wind and consist of three actions: the swell of the water, its crest and curl, and its collapse. The work occurs when the water falls, for rock is moved against rock when energy is dispersed from the collapsed wave. As dancing white water splashes into foam, broken rock is thrown onto larger blocks of underlying bedrock. Over time the larger blocks are broken into smaller stone.

SEA WAVE: SWELL, CURL AND COLLAPSE

THE NATIVE ROCK

When the bedrock below the wave is sedimentary, the broken pieces eventually become smoother and flatter, and a shingle beach is formed. When the bedrock below the wave is metamorphic, the pieces become smoother and irregular. When the bedrock below the wave is igneous, the pieces become smoother and rounder.

Both metamorphic and igneous rock form boulder beaches with stones larger than 6 inches across. These wear down to cobble beaches with stones 2-6 inches and then to pebble beaches with stones 1/4-2 inches. All beaches, no matter what type of rock, will erode to sand beaches eventually. The particles of sand are quartz grains left at the beach head while the other minerals are dispersed as silt, clay, and mud into deeper water and carried to the continental shelf.

SEA WAVE EROSION

Newcomers to the ocean are eager to learn about the tides. Passing over the bridge at the Narrows to the island, they are often surprised to see the mud flats of the ocean floor. We say that the tide "goes out" for six hours and the tide "comes in" for six hours. These periods of "moving water" are called ebb and flow. Short rest periods throw the time of the tides off each day by about one hour. High tide of 2:00 P.M. today will result in a high tide tomorrow of about 3:00 P.M.

THE NATIVE ROCK

Actually, the water does not move in or out. The oceans bulge by the gravitational pull of the moon and sun and by the centrifugal force of the earth's rotation. The earth rotates under the bulges. The delay of about one hour a day relates to the moon's position in its monthly revolution of 28 days around the earth. When the sun and moon align, the gravitational pull is very strong and the tidal differences are more pronounced.

Tidal differences are described in both a horizontal and vertical range. At headlands, bluffs and cliffs, the tide may never be horizontal, only vertical. In shallow bays, coves, beaches and flats, the tides may be more horizontal than vertical.

The horizontal range is the distance between low and high tide marks where the ocean floor is exposed. The floor may be ledge or sand or mud. It is a distance that you can walk.

The vertical range measures the difference between low and high tide in depth of water. The depth is about ten feet on the island; however, the Bay of Fundy in Canada to the northeast shows a vertical range of 50 feet. The horizontal range there is over a mile. Such extreme ranges give a feature called a tidal bore where special cautions need to be given to visitors, for it is possible for the unsuspecting to become stranded on sand bars in deep water when the tide comes in.

Without a daily tide chart, the tide can be determined roughly by a short study of the shoreline. When the tide is coming in, the waves pass over dry rock or beach, that is, if it is a dry day!

Obviously, on a rainy day, this observation will not work. When the tide goes out, the shoreline is left wet from the sea water. Watch carefully for several minutes, for not all waves are of the same size. One wave may break far ahead of the others, which may wet the zone you are observing.

Likewise, along headlands, the swells that break vertically are not each one the same. Several small swells may break in succession followed by a more powerful one. Victims have been picked up and carried out by undertows currents that pull them beneath the water to resurface far from shore. On rocks at or near the water's edge, take care!

Ocean Drive on the Park Loop Road in Acadia is a very good field trip. From Schooner Head Overlook to Hunter's Beach Head, there are many features carved by the sea for you to explore. Plan the trip at low tide to see interesting

THE NATIVE ROCK

features on the shoreline, for you will see a wave-cut sea cave; a sea chasm; sand, cobble, and boulder beaches; and headlands. You will find features of eroded batholiths, such as shatter zones and diabase dikes, and features of the glacier, such as erratics and chatter marks, in the tidal zone. A planned field geology guide follows, but first read the information about compass points.

What do we say about the rocks? The ancient Avalonian land ship! The carbon and concretion remnants! The generations of granite! The intervals of intrusion! The transforming earth! What a mystery, this earth, for those with eyes to see!

DIABASE DIKES THROUGH SOUTH BUBBLE MOUNTAIN

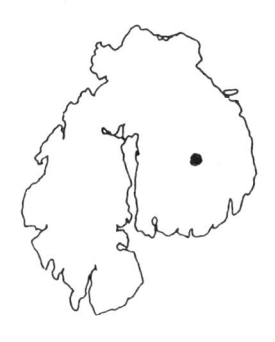

THE NATIVE ROCK

Compass Points

Directions for Determining Compass Points: To help you follow the field geology guide, you will need to know North from South. If you have a compass, take it with you. However, you can learn to tell the approximate points of the compass if you know what time of day it is. You may need a watch but not a compass! Learn to do this on bright and sunny days, but as you become proficient, you may have good success on cloudy days as well.

Let us pretend it is noon. Pretend to stand with your face under the sun so that your face is full of light and warmth. Your shadow will be behind you at a 90 degree angle to your body. You are facing south, and the sun is at its highest overhead, but at 44 degrees North Latitude, which is MDI's position on the globe, it will not be in the apex of the sky, that is, not in the center of the sky directly over your head.

N

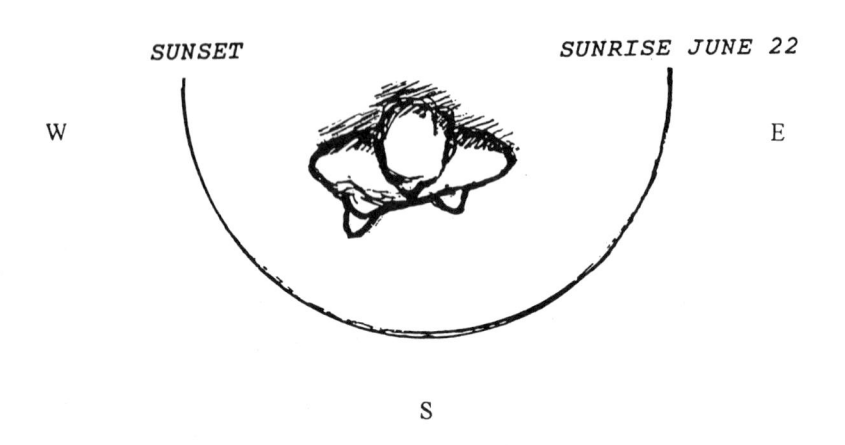

SUNSET   *SUNRISE JUNE 22*

W   E

S

12 NOON

Now pretend your right shoulder is pointing west and your left shoulder is pointing east. Turn your body in the direction of your right shoulder and you are facing west. Turn your body in the direction of your left shoulder and you are facing east.

THE NATIVE ROCK

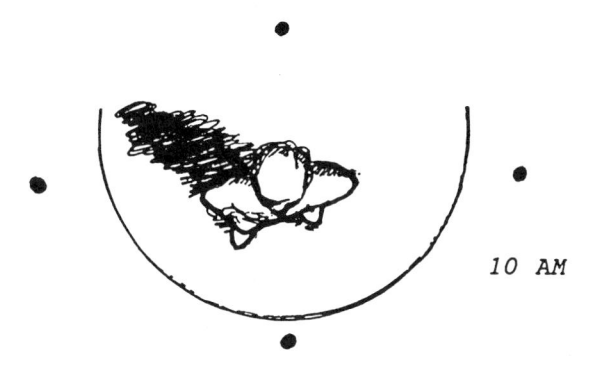

10 AM

Depending on the hour before noon, the sun will appear to the east. Make an estimate of the sun's position in the sky from morning to noon. In the morning, your shadow will be long and point to the west.

Conversely, in the afternoon, the sun will appear to the west. Again, estimate the sun's position in the sky from noon to afternoon. In the afternoon, your shadow will be long and point to the east.

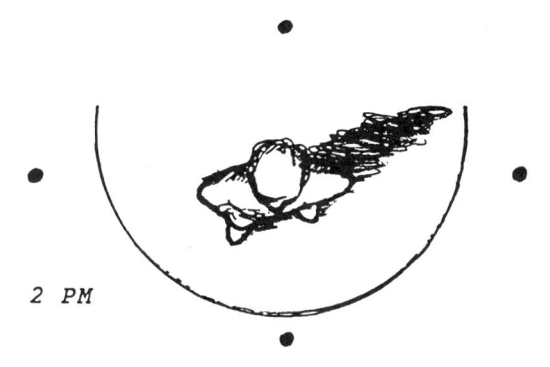

2 PM

Turn opposite south and you will be facing north. No sun will fall upon your face unless you tilt your face back. Sun will fall on the top of your head. At noon, you will not be able to see your shadow when you face north even though it is before you unless you tilt your head down to see it, for your shadow will be its shortest.

After practice, you may be able to find the brightest and warmest place in the southern sky to put your face even on cloudy days. Directions of north, east, south, and west will be given for your trip on Ocean Drive. Schooner Head Overlook, your first stop, is a good spot to try to find the compass points.

THE NATIVE ROCK

Code of Geological Conduct

1. Foster an interest in geologic sites and their conservation.

2. Observe and photograph the rocks: Do not collect them.

3. Be careful on cliffs and rocky shorelines.

4. On coastal trails, know tidal conditions.

5. Stay on the trails:
    1. Fragile plants are easily trampled.
    2. Ticks carry lyme disease.
    3. Wildlife appreciates its own space.

6. Respect wildlife: Observe quietly from a distance

7. Respect private landowners whose properties border Acadia National Park or the island's shoreline.

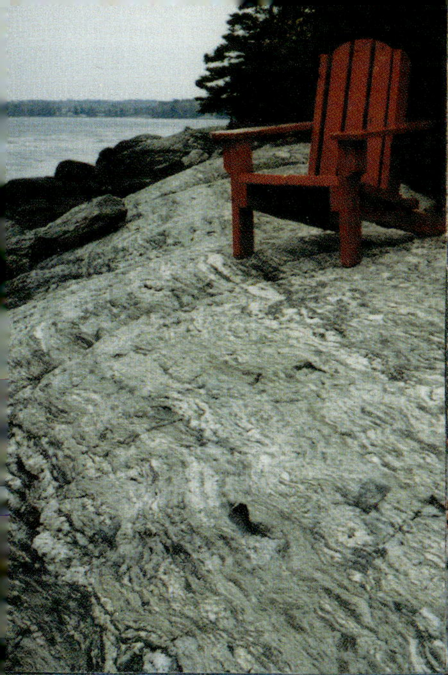
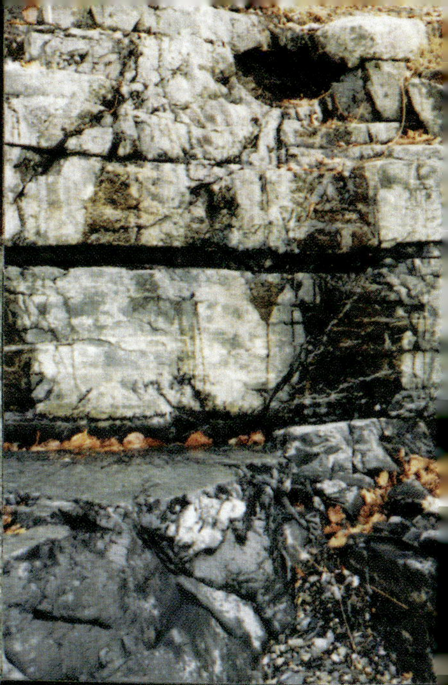
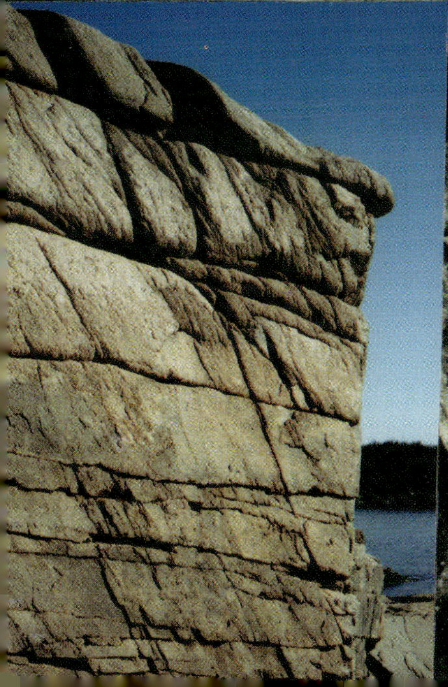
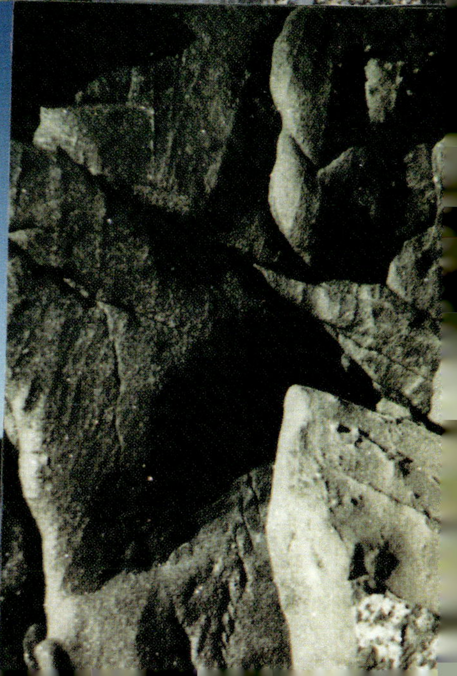

MOUNT DESERT ISLAND BEDROCK

Top Left: AVALONIAN LANDSHIP
Avalonian metamorphic bedrock, Indian Point, Blagden Preserve

Top Right: CARBON AND CONCRETION REMNANTS
Bar Harbor Series sediments, The Ovens, Salisbury Cove

Bottom Left: FIRST GENERATION GRANITE
Cadillac granite bedrock, Ocean Drive, Acadia National Park

Bottom Right: INTERVAL OF INTRUSION
Black dike formation, Schooner Head, Acadia National Park

THE NATIVE ROCK

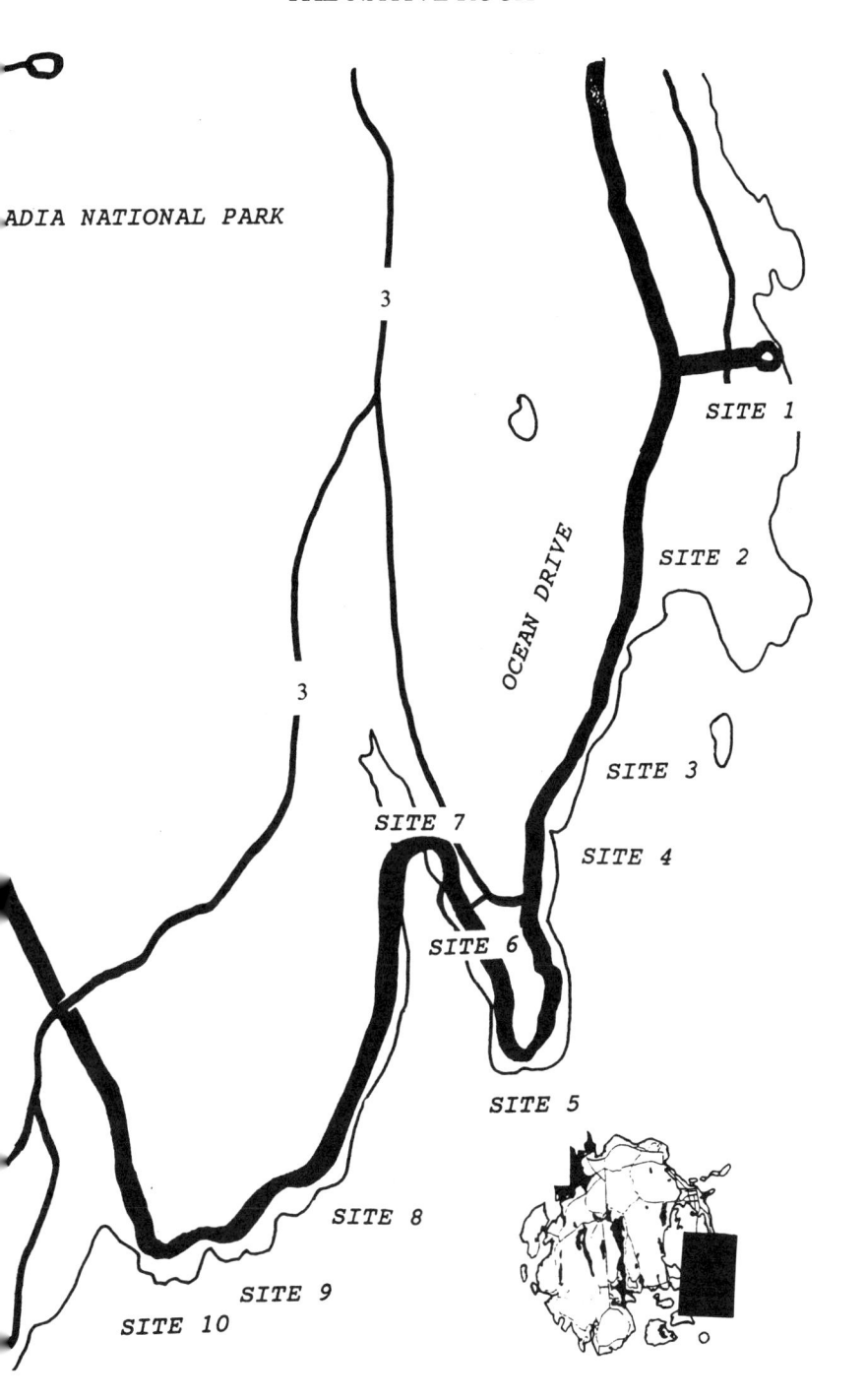

THE NATIVE ROCK

Field Geology

The following guide provides plans for six field trips to areas of geologic interest. All involve walking over uneven ground, most include some climbing over rocks. Good walking shoes are suggested. Take a sweatshirt with you. A snack and drink in a fanny pack is a good idea. Take your camera, also binoculars and compass if you have them. Be sure to take this guide with you. After completing the hikes, you should congratulate yourself: you will be able to identify igneous, sedimentary, and metamorphic rock and geologic features on your own, not only here on MDI but elsewhere on earth.

Field Trip 1 - Ocean Drive on the Park Loop Road in Acadia National Park, 5-6 hours, easy walking with some difficult climbs, low tide is best so dividing this trip in two trips may be a good idea, drive by car to 10 sites all close to the park loop road and all with suitable parking areas, early morning hours give best light for photos.

Site 1: Drive to Schooner Head Overlook. Walk to the southern end of the parking lot to an outcropping of rock which was blasted for the road into the parking area. Look carefully at the cut rock and you will see fragments of Bar Harbor Series sedimentary rock in a granite matrix. The granite is a part of the batholith that is the bedrock of the eastern half of the island, which includes Champlain Mountain to your northwest. The granite at your feet is not as pink as the granite to the center of the batholith. Here at the boundary it has been influenced by the sedimentary rock. This is a contact zone between the two rock types.

SHATTER ZONE

THE NATIVE ROCK

Turn around and walk in a northerly direction. The headland that you see is Schooner Head and the beautiful home on it is privately owned. The cobble beach between the headland and the parking lot was worked by sea waves since the glacier receded under 14,000 years ago.

Look to the north and east and you will see Frenchman Bay and across the bay high elevations. The mountains on the mainland are made of granite, and they are part of a granite zone that extends from southwest of Mt. Desert Island to the Canadian border to the northeast. To the southeast is Schoodic Peninsula.

Take the pathway to the very rocky shore. Work your way down to the lower rocks over the contact zone. Choose your footing carefully. At the low rocks, turn and walk to the south. The waves have thrown stone against the weak joints in the shatter zone, breaking away the sedimentary from the igneous rock. Climbing over the rocks in this area is difficult, but your exploration will yield several unexpected surprises.

FRACTURED SHATTER ZONE

THE NATIVE ROCK

If you are not able to make this difficult climb, retrace your steps to your car for your drive to Site 2, but if you decide to venture on, pass over the fractured shatter zone. Walk southward and start your climb up the other side to the pathway. Take your time. The ocean water has stained the rocks which at first glance all appear dark gray and black, many of which are very slippery.

Look carefully, noting instead of color, both shape and texture. Blocks of granite have eroded away to expose a diabase formation. The folds of magma can still be seen, even drips where the magma hardened over 200 million years ago. How protected it was inside the earth! You can read its fine details! The wall of rock that enclosed it was imprinted against it. Note the erosion to those portions of the diabase that have been exposed to weathering for a long time.

DIABASE FORMATION

THE NATIVE ROCK

Site 2. Drive to Sand Beach. Take the stairway that leads down to the beach. Note the pink granite ledges to the southwest. Note the shoal, a ledge covered by high tide, to the southeast. The shoal is named Old Soaker and is part of an underwater ledge that made the ocean bottom of the cove into the shape of a bowl. The broken bits of seashells can not drift offshore to the continental shelf as occurs on most beaches. The debris builds up in the cove. Fall and winter storms move the sand and shell occasionally to the shoal and ledge, but by spring the particles return to make up the beach.

Walk to the east across the beach. Examine a handful of the beach particles. You will see small pieces of green sea urchin spine, white clamshell, blue mussel shell, and quartz grains.

The headland in front of you is called Great Head. Just before reaching it, examine some of the rocks at the east side. You will see that you are in the contact zone again. You will see broken fragments of sedimentary rock within granite, stained with rust from the iron minerals. At the shoreline at low tide you will see blocks of shatter zone material worn smooth by the sea waves.

SAND BEACH & GREAT HEAD

Climb the pathway that leads up Great Head. The hike around the headland is an interesting rock walk over the shatter zone with occasional masses of dike material and diorite that make up a good part of the floor of Frenchman Bay. A hike just high enough to get a good view of Sand Beach is recommended. After

THE NATIVE ROCK

reaching the halfway mark, look northwest to see the Beehive, a large block of Cadillac granite that was carved by the glacier. Note its steep south side. When the glacier froze into the south side, it plucked or quarried large rock blocks from the granite upon its moving forward. Note the brackish lagoon behind the dune grass of the beach. Each year the lagoon fills more and more with sand, silt, clay and mud, all of which washes down from the higher elevations.

THE BEEHIVE

Site 3. Drive on to Thunder Hole. Everyone expects to find the sea chasm booming! Actually, it booms very well during fall and winter storms when the surf splashes onto the cars on the loop road above Thunder Hole. The best time to see waves is at mid-tide. The best time to see the boulders that cut the chasm is low tide. This chasm was formed when sea waves pushed rock into a weak fracture that runs along the coastline at this point. The boom of Thunder Hole is caused by compressed air when waves hit the entrance of a small cave at the head of the chasm. At low tide, the waves can not close off the entrance. At high tide, waves are above the entrance. At mid-tide, the waves can compress air.

THE NATIVE ROCK

THUNDER HOLE

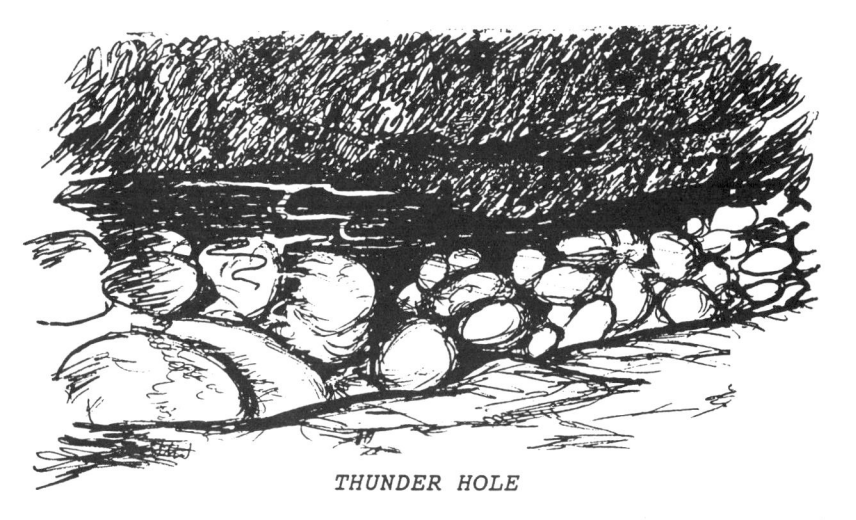

If you walk northerly from Thunder Hole back in the direction of Sand Beach, you can spot this fracture or fault line. The granite has deteriorated along the fault line to a crumbly material that could be knocked out with a claw hammer. The fault line exists because of the pounding the rock has received for the thousands of years since the coastline rebounded after the glacier. Without doubt, the weakness was predestined by the breaking up of the continental plates and made weaker still by the glacier that moved over the island in more recent geologic time.

FAULTLINE

THE NATIVE ROCK

Site 4. Drive next to Monument Cove Parking Area a short distance ahead. Walk to the shorepath where you can get a good look at the boulder beach below. These are granite stones smoothed by rolling and grinding, one against another as the waves turn them over. If you climb down to the beach, you can hear the grinding under the waves. Note the granite cliffs that are providing rock for the beach. Note the difference in the color, texture, and shape of the cliffs that are above high tide mark with the appearance of the granite that is washed by the sea.

Site 5. Drive next to Otter Point Parking Area, .3 mile beyond Otter Cliffs. The cliff over which you have driven is 110 feet over the water and is a busy spot in summer. At Otter Point you can see the same features that you can see at the Cliff and more!

Walk to the shoreline closest to the parking lot. You will see that you are in the shatter zone again! If you stay southward and eastward of the point, you will see large blocks of the Bar Harbor Series melted into the Cadillac granite, and something more! For in many places, the heat and pressure of the molten igneous rock metamorphosed the sedimentary rock into pockets of quartzite.

First, note the black stain and red rust on the rocks of the Bar Harbor Series at the shoreline. Second, note the light lavender and gray layers of recently exposed sedimentary rock, and third, the alteration into brittle pale green, light orange, lavender and pale pink quartzite.

QUARTZITE ARROW

THE NATIVE ROCK

One pocket occurs on a high bluff where an arrow-shaped, pale green quartzite hardened in pink granite. This block was once layers of Bar Harbor Series sedimentary that dropped into the hot magma. Another pocket occurs under the "arrow." It is a pale green well where the rock has been eroded or quarried and which is now filled with water.

In the bedrock, there is a long vein called a pegmatite. Its chief mineral is feldspar. It is about 10-12 inches wide in places. The metamorphosed rock had become so hot that it had started to melt into a granite when instead, it cooled. If enough time of heat and pressure had been allowed, the minerals would have regrouped to an igneous rock. The pegmatite vein has narrow walls of both quartzite and pegmatite feldspar.

PEGMATITE VEIN

If you have difficulty locating the pegmatite vein, look instead for an eroded gravel bank where a number of large pink Cadillac granite boulders, some 8-9 feet across, have dropped onto the ledges. The boulders are erratics carried by ice and deposited in glacial till. In more recent years, the bank has been eroded by storm waves. In front of the gravel bank, you will see the large quartzite deposit with its pegmatite vein.

THE NATIVE ROCK

ERRATICS

Look to the sea as you stand by the pegmatite vein. You will see a high block of rock that has resisted plate tectonics, the glacier, and the ocean storm waves. It has quite a story to tell. Climb upon it and take a look. On the north side of this amazing rock, you will see just how a pegmatite forms. You will see how hot and viscous solutions shoot through the rock, how they find the weak places in the layers, how they reinforce themselves and become wider, and how they fill thin feldspar walls until they appear as the pegmatite vein among the pale quartzite. We do not know how long this action takes. Perhaps it happened in seconds, perhaps in millions of years. Look closely for the story is written in short sentences and the print is small!

PEGMATITE SUTURES

THE NATIVE ROCK

Along the ledges to the northwest side of the point, you will find glacial scratches and a scant trace of polish on the rocks near the shoreline. To the northwest of Otter Point, you can see Otter Cove, where you will drive next. Note the glacial meltwater channel high between Cadillac and Dorr Mountains. The glacier moved from the north over the mountains toward you in the south. At the height of the glacier, ice was perhaps a mile or more thick over what you recognize as mountain tops today.

The glacier had within its layers of ice, rivers that flowed on it, through it, and below it. The meltwater channel that you see was carved by a glacial river that flowed under the thick ice to the south. Otter Cove is its resulting feature.

In the cove there is a shoal which is covered at high tide. It is made of pink granite and has resisted the ice that flowed over it. You may have your chance to hike to this shoal from a future stop at the Causeway. Note the stone bridge over the Causeway to the northwest.

OTTER COVE

THE NATIVE ROCK

Site 6. Drive next to the Fabbri Memorial. The parking area provides an overlook of Otter Cove. Stand on the high ground just in front of the path that leads down to the shoreline. Look westerly and you will see the other side of the cove. Across the cove along the shoreline, you will see a gravel till deposit, at the bottom of which, you will see a blue deposit of clay. Even from this distance, the deposit is large enough to show up on a photo from a 35mm camera; with a larger or zoom lens you can take a better picture.

BLUE CLAY DEPOSIT

Take the path to the bluffs below. Here you will see glacial polish and fine glacial scratches running roughly N-S. Look north toward the Causeway Imagine an ice mass one mile high over Cadillac Mountain of 1530 feet.

Site 7. Drive on next to the Causeway. If you park on the side of the loop road you can take a closer look at the inlet to the north which has a muddy flat at low tide and a full body of salt water at high tide.

50

THE NATIVE ROCK

On the south side of the road, you will see a small pebble beach and a till deposit to the east, your left, as you look out to sea. The till deposit with its underlying blue clay that you saw from the Fabbri Memorial is to the west, your right. Please be careful of traffic as you explore on the Causeway.

Walk easterly around the cove and note the boulders of Cadillac granite carried to the cove by the glacier. Especially note the shape, for unlike the boulders of Monument Cove which have ground themselves into circular and oval spheres, many of these have one or more flattened surfaces. These are boulders that were carried along the bottom ice. They became flattened as they sanded the rock over which they slid. Many of their flattened surfaces show scratches on them as they were in turn scratched by smaller rock caught between the moving surface and the bedrock.

If the tide allows, climb up on the second of the two shoals that lies about 100 feet offshore. You will see the carving of the ice in a very dramatic way. Curved mounds of solid granite show cusp-like cracks called chatter marks. They will remind you perhaps of the marks on a scoop of hard ice cream made by the metal scoop. How long did it take? How fast was the ice moving? The great weight of the ice sheared rock here, perhaps in seconds by a sudden shift in its enormous mass. Note the N-S running glacial scratches over the rock. After all these years, they can still be seen!

SHOALS IN OTTER COVE

THE NATIVE ROCK

Site 8. Drive next to Western Point. Here you will park in one of three pull-over areas which can accommodate a total of 10-12 cars. Walk to a pathway through the bushes and to a grassy area above the point. A stone stairway will lead you to a view but not to the coastline safely. Visitors have made their way to the point in an effort to explore its beauty. The best way down to the shoreline is below the second of the three parking areas.

On the point you will see a dike of diabase material that is imprinted or stamped with a crossline pattern. It was created when uplifting magma hit an overlying rock, which has since been quarried either by nature or by man.

IMPRINTED DIABASE

Below on the beach, walk to the east and you will find in the bedrock a struggle between once molten pink granite and black diabase now frozen in time. The one mass in the other will remind you perhaps of an ice cream swirl. (Peach and licorice flavors, although on a wet day, perhaps, strawberry and dark chocolate syrup better describe the colors!) The boulders and cobbles here are of both igneous rocks. Note the lumpy roundness of the diabase and the more even roundness of the granite.

THE NATIVE ROCK

WESTERN POINT

As you walk near the high tide mark in this area, keep your eyes peeled for an exposure of granite that has crumbled. It will appear greenish and is cracked and crumbled over a space 10-12 feet wide. Its dark mineral has weathered to a greenish color, its feldspar has the softness of clay, and its quartz grains can be removed with your fingertip. This is a severely fractured zone. If you stand in front of it on the beach, you may feel the shoreline under your feet shake whenever waves hit the large boulders, 8-10 feet across, at the shoreline at mid-tide. The battering this zone has taken over the years is claiming the bluff. In time a chasm like the one at Thunder Hole may be formed here. In short time the loop road above it may have to be repaired!

Site 9. Drive to Little Hunter's Beach. The parking spot on the right hand side of the loop road holds 3-4 cars only. You are encouraged to stop here if you can, however, to see a big mound of cobbles that form a beach between two high bluffs. Look to the south and out to sea. To the west are steep, fractured bluffs of shatter zone where diorite and sedimentary rock have hardened together. To the east there is a large exposure of diabase.

A walk along the high bluffs to your left will provide good views of the shatter zone. Quartzite can be seen too. Explore around a bit, and find the dikes of diabase. Color is disguised because of weathering and staining. The rust red powder in some areas is from the iron oxides in the sedimentary rocks, the black is from decayed vegetation that has run in water from the land, and the darkened rocks below in the tidal zone are discolored from the sea.

THE NATIVE ROCK

Watch for texture and shape. The granite is grained and rounded, the dike material is dense and broken into blocks, the sedimentary layers can be identified, and the quartzite is brittle and fractured along irregular lines.

Site 10. Drive to Hunter's Beach Head Overlook. You are on a steep cliff 100 feet above the ocean. The parking area holds 8-10 cars. Note to the west the ledges and cliffs of Sea Cliff Drive. This drive is not within Acadia National Park. It is a road within the Village of Seal Harbor. Along the top of the cliff halfway between the overlook and the point, you can just barely see a high white prominence of the quartz vein described in this guide.

QUARTZ VEIN AT SEACLIFF DRIVE

The cliff rocks under you are made up of igneous and sedimentary rock in a shatter zone between those two bodies. On the blasted rock surfaces to the north across the parking area and loop road, you will see the contact. Be careful of traffic if you go closely to see the infusion and veins.

Although you have now completed Ocean Drive, you have only seen a small part of the beauty of Mount Desert Island. More explorations await you!

THE NATIVE ROCK

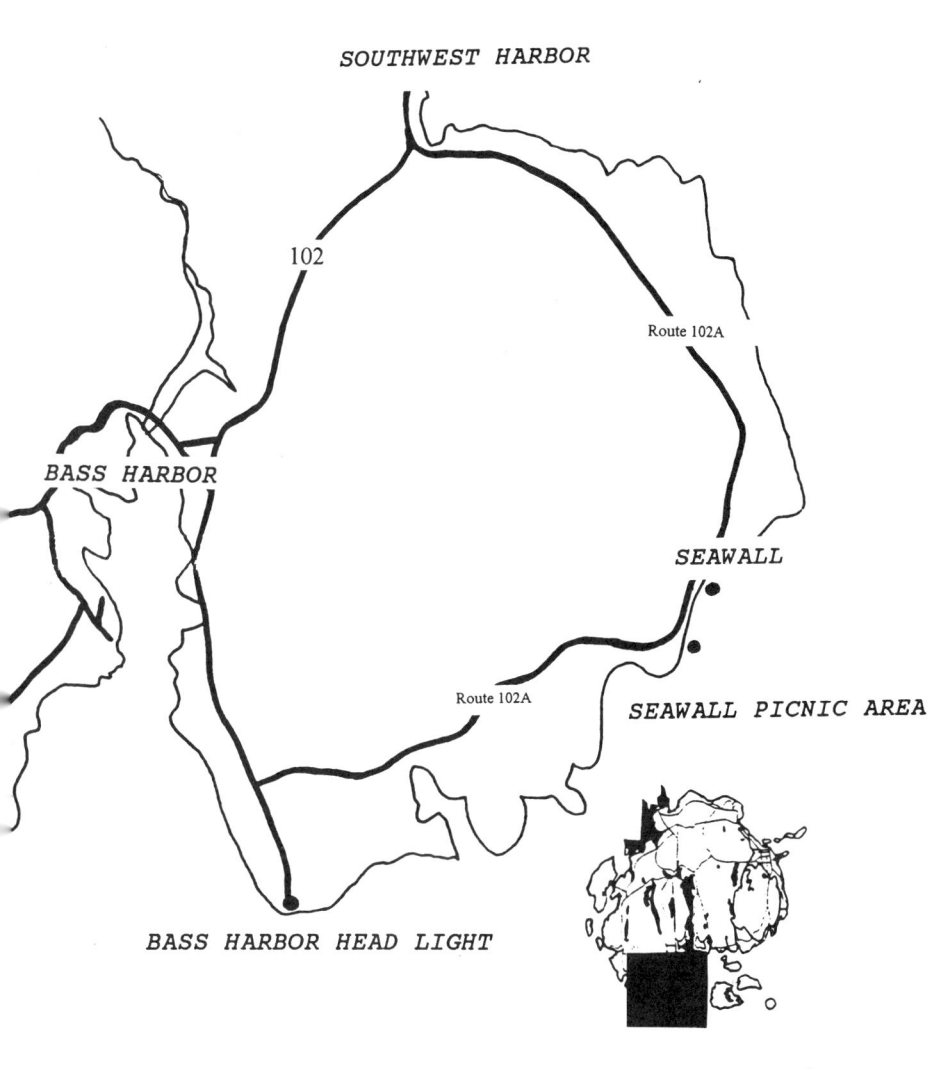

Field Trip 2 - Seawall and Bass Harbor Head, 1-2 hrs., drive by car to three sites, low tide best, easy walking over boulder beaches with one moderately difficult climb on stairs and ledges.

Site 1. Drive to Seawall on route map. Park along roadside on the cobbles. Caution: drive in and out of parking space carefully. (You'll park on many sedimentary cobbles trucked in to secure the road.) Walk southward to the beach of cobbles and boulders.

THE NATIVE ROCK

Walk down to the low or mid-tidal water where the bedrock material has been rolled onto the beach from the ledges underwater. The bedrock at Seawall is a special pink granite that has been altered at its surface. Near the center of the seawall, you will see a ledge that is about 90 feet long and nearly as wide. Walk out if tide permits. The granite under your feet has been disturbed by tuff layers of ash that fell from an ancient volcano onto its surface. The hot material that fell included some large blocks of crust which sank into the mix. The thick hot coating seared the granite bedrock. The granite was reheated and its minerals were able to regroup. You will see pods of quartz along with large feldspar and mica crystals. Accompanying these you may find the faint blue-green color of the mineral microline, which though not quality gem is a beautiful color.

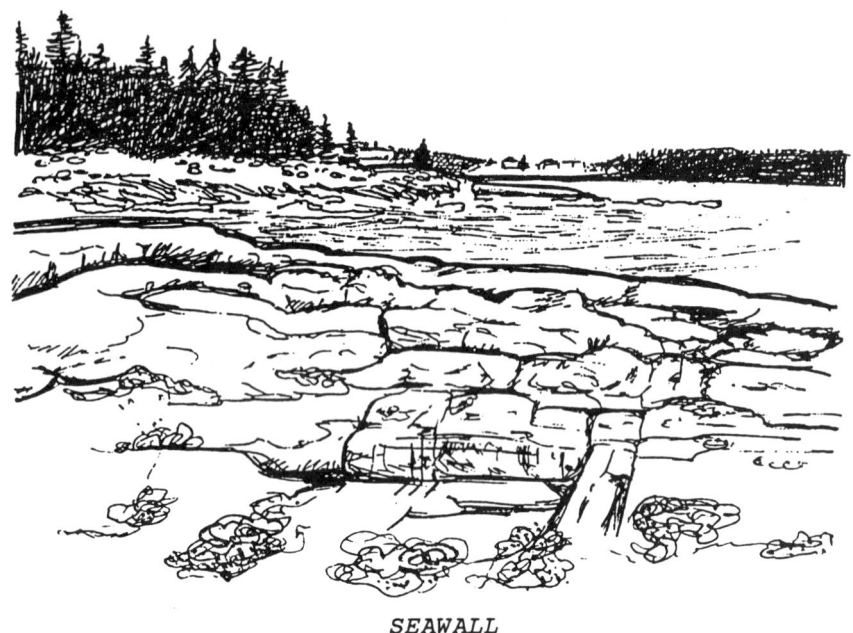

SEAWALL

As you walk over the ledge, note the glacial cutting that has left flat, horizontal surfaces, once smoother but now rough. At the far end of the ledge, turn around and look back toward shore. You will see a deposit of breccia on your right which is very interesting. In the material are large boulders and hundreds of little holes where gases have escaped. Near the base are granite bedrock blocks that have squirmed into thin sheets from the weight and heat of the volcanic layers. Through and under the tuff and breccia, a liquid mineral has run over the thin granite sheets and blocks. The hardened syrup is yellow and red. Once there may have been much more of it, but it has been eroded away by the sea.

THE NATIVE ROCK

TUFF & BRECCIA

Look at the various rock types on the beach. You will see all types because the glacier dropped erratics here. The bedrock is pink granite. You will find boulders that appear to have the "measles," which are stains from the regrouping of hematite, an iron mineral in the rock, the granite from the central edge and surrounding bedrock.

THE NATIVE ROCK

Walk about 200 feet to the right as you face the sea toward some large dark rocks that are higher than the surrounding beach stones at low or mid-tide. You will cross the beach stones of mostly granite into the rocks of the Cranberry Island Series. Soon you will see three dark diabase dikes that run northeasterly near the beach head. Two are narrow almost at the head of the beach, and one is 3-4 feet wide and runs from the beach head to large rocks about 5-6 feet high. These dikes belong to the earlier set of dikes that are found running northeasterly. The rock has a more lumpy and plastic shape to it than the latter set that runs northwesterly. The rock hardened when magma shot upwards to seal cracks left by crustal stretching. The cracks may have occurred when the continents separated about 225 million years ago.

DIKES AT SEAWALL

Since North America and Africa were first parted, the cracks formed between the two. This separation did not take place here at the 44 degree North Latitude but somewhere near the equator of the earth as Pangea moved northerly. The magma came from the mantle of that part of the world, not from mantle of the earth below the crust in this part of the world. Since the mantle is molten and is churned by convection currents, we might ask ourselves if there is any difference.

THE NATIVE ROCK

Site 2. Next drive a short distance to Seawall Picnic Area. Park your car near the middle section of the beach. Face the sea and then walk to the left. The beach section to the left of the middle of the picnic area has an outcropping near high tide mark of tuff and breccia, probably formed under an earlier sea. In time they were compressed into thick layers of the Cranberry Island Series of sedimentary rock. You will see different rock types included in the mix.

Along the beach not far from the high tide mark, there are exposures of an underlying, coarse grained, pink granite. It appears from under the Cranberry Island Series.

Also in the ledges of bedrock that are outcropped at the head of the beach, you will find concretions or rounded shapes that have weathered to a greenish material. The eroded centers may remind you of decayed wood with many small cavities. In the area of the Ovens in Salisbury Cove, there are concretions like these. The material has not been identified; however, it is not unlike limonite, an iron oxide, which is a waste material like this when a rich iron-bearing rock is smelted. Concretions often contain fossils so perhaps the green cavities were once plant or sea life.

Walking south and west around a point of land, you will find an interesting deposit of tuff and breccia that has been overlain with an ancient lava flow. You will see the pocketed surface of the lava flow that resembles hundreds of miniature craters. Evidentially, the glacier did not carve it away. If the crust was depressed during the Ice Age, the area of the Cranberry Island Series may have been under a shallow sea which may have floated the ice sheet over the lava flows both here and on the Cranberry Isles. The flows are remarkably well-preserved in some places. If you are interested, it may be worth the trip to Little Cranberry Island, where on its northern shoreline, there are good flow lines of the extrusive lava. On the northern beaches of Little Cranberry Island, there are smooth and shiny black pebbles and cobbles which have gray spots of ash that fell into the extrusive lava flow.

If you continue to walk west, you will enter a cove where there is a rich accumulation of cobblestones. At one time the Seawall beach that you first visited was greater than it is now, but many boulders were taken away for construction purposes. Visitors have also taken stone in the past; however, since the area belongs now to the park, it is better protected. The cobblestone beach in the cove ahead has not been disturbed.

THE NATIVE ROCK

Site 3. Drive next to Bass Harbor Head Light. The lighthouse is operated by the United States Coast Guard, and although you can not enter the facility, you may explore those grounds not fenced off to you. The climb to the rocks under the lighthouse begins to your left from the parking area as you face the lighthouse. The short walk through the woods leads to a wooden stairway with rail. Climb down carefully to the rocks if you feel able.

The large blocks of granite are a pink color and have a granular texture. The Bass Harbor granite is an unexplained type. There are other outcroppings of bedrock in addition to the Bass Harbor granite that differ from the larger accumulations of Southwest Harbor, Somesville, and Cadillac granite. It is thought that the little bubbles of pink granite that surround the island are cupolas of magma that formed later than the recognized Southwest Harbor, Somesville, and Cadillac types. Perhaps they were formed when the roof of sedimentary and metamorphic layers melted into or fell into the Cadillac granite.

At low tide you will see more lava flow below the pink, granular granite. If you climb to these rocks, you will see small holes that contained gases at one time. The many broken cavities are large enough to hold nickels and dimes.

The view of the lighthouse from the shore is photogenic because you are looking into a northern sky. A bluer sky on a clear day can not be found.

BASS HARBOR HEAD LIGHTHOUSE

THE NATIVE ROCK

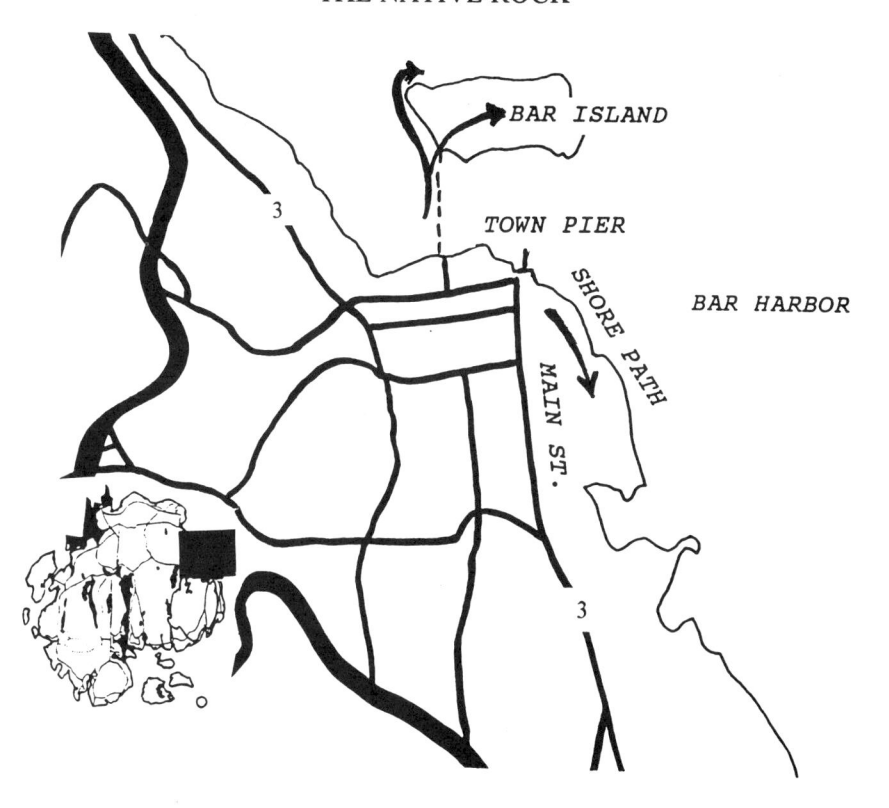

Field Trip 3 - Bar Harbor Village, Shore Path and Bar Island

Site 1. Shore Path, 1-2 hrs., easy walking over groomed path, along shoreline with short climbs down to the beach, length of walk under 1 mile, medium to low tide suggested

From your intown parking spot, walk to the Town Beach adjacent to the Town Pier. As you cross above the stone wall in front of the Bar Harbor Inn, note the glacial scratches on an exposed ledge at the northeast end of the beach. The scratches show up best in an outcrop of diorite, but they can be seen on the Bar Harbor Series sedimentary layers also.

A little further on, the layers of the Bar Harbor Series appear as flat and rusted blocks. The rust is iron oxide, red powder from hematite.

Along the path are lovely, white birch trees and on the right a number of coarse grained white granite boulders in the lawn. These 6-8 feet high boulders are erratics left by the glacier. After passing the trees and erratics, take a climb

THE NATIVE ROCK

down to the beach. The stones on the beach have been worn smooth and flat. The beach is called a shingle beach because of the shape of its sandstones.

You need walk only a short distance back in the direction of the Town Pier to examine a sea stack, a block of sedimentary rock that has resisted erosion. This stack of sedimentary layers was called Pulpit Rock in the 1800's.

SEA STACK

Continue on your walk. The offshore islands are made up of Bar Harbor Series and diorite sills and their northern boundaries are lower than their southern boundaries due to the tilting of the layers.

Soon you will see on your left a large erratic called Balance Rock on a ledge of sandstone. This ten-foot granite boulder stood on end until it toppled in a storm during the 1970's.

THE NATIVE ROCK

BALANCE ROCK

As you continue on your walk, feel free to examine the rocks. Both on the beach and in the stone walls that support the Shore Path, you will see different rock types. Use this guide to help your identification. The shoreline will present on the next point of land bedrock outcroppings. Explore these rocks and you will find diorite and Bar Harbor Series. A gray dike runs through the outcropping. It has eroded more slowly than the bedrock so it is higher by about a foot. It has a curving ribbon shape to it and can be spotted in the water at low tide.

At one place very close to the path, a sill of feldspar has eroded. It looks like a coating of thick white paint. The waves wash over the sedimentary layers smoothly because the angle of their incline is agreeable with the washing sea. Several small quartz veins can be found near these rocks.

One very large block of diorite bedrock has been worked by the sea. Below it, many rounded cobbles of diorite have piled up with the sandstones at the head of the beach. Note the colors of these rocks both in bedrock and in the beach.

THE NATIVE ROCK

GRAY DIKE

To complete the walk, take the path at the end to your right into the village. You will end up on Main Street. Walk to your right to the intersection of Cottage and Main Streets. From there you can see the ocean. Walk down the hill to the Town Pier. As you pass the shops and restaurants, you will smell the coffee, chocolate, and hot blueberry pie. Sooner or later, you will be right back where you started your trip.

Site 2. Bar Island, 2-3 hrs., easy walking over a firm sand bar with occasional scrambles over boulders and ledges, under 3 miles of walking, low tide a must, bar very windy so hooded sweatshirt is advised on colder days

THE NATIVE ROCK

Park along a street close to the bar. Never park on the bar! Walk across the sand bar, noting the pebble beach of the Bar Harbor Series. As you approach the island, veer off to the left and start around the shoreline. You will pass rocks that belong to the Bar Harbor Series and outcrops of diorite. Underfoot not far from the high tide mark, you will see ledges with glacial scratches. Chatter marks can be seen as well.

Soon you will turn to the right and start a short walk along the northern shoreline. Look for the feldspar dikes up ahead. They stand 1-4 feet higher than the surrounding rock. Look ahead along the shoreline and you will spot an erratic shaped like a big Dutch wooden shoe. It is Lucerne granite resting upon diorite. It is not as well known as Balance Rock but just as beautiful!

ERRATIC

THE NATIVE ROCK

Return to the bar over which you crossed in the beginning of the walk. Instead of returning to Bar Harbor, start the pathway up and over Bar Island to the hilltop on its southern end. As you climb the hill of about 300 feet, you will see ledges of broken diorite underfoot. At the top you will have a good view of the harbor.

Look at the boats and notice their bows. Their bows point into the wind, and the wind is usually from the south into the harbor. The water is sheltered by the stone block causeway that was built from Bald Porcupine Island toward the Shore Path with an opening left for passage.

The view from the hilltop includes mountains: to your left-right, Champlain Huguenot Head followed by the U-shaped valley, Dorr, the long North Ridge of Cadillac (the highest), and behind Cadillac some of Sargent Mountain, and to the hard right, Great Hill.

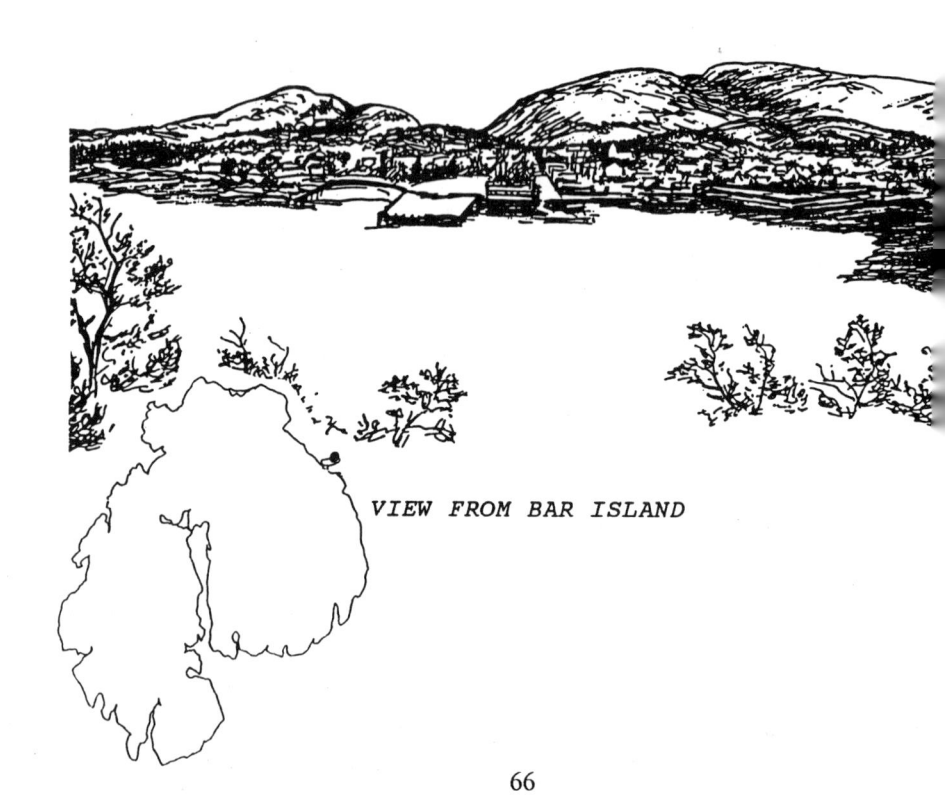

VIEW FROM BAR ISLAND

THE NATIVE ROCK

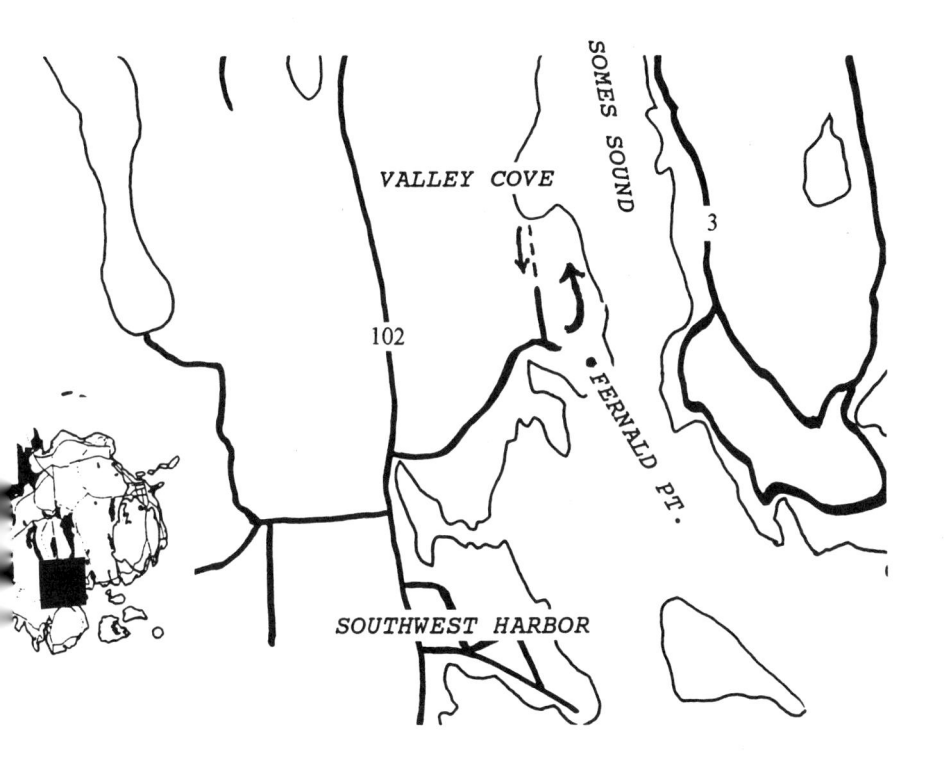

Field Trip 4 - Flying Mountain and Valley Cove, 2-3 hrs., moderate to difficult climb to an elevation of 300 feet and sharp descent, under 3 miles of hiking, excellent views of Somes Sound, low tide in order to see rocks on the shore of Valley Cove after the descent from the mountain

Start the climb from the parking lot. The first of the hike will take you under old conifers to a rocky ledge. Climbing is at times steep. You will pull yourself up over shatter zone material to a large outcropping of a dark dike. Stand on the wide flat black rock at the top and enjoy the view. Look to the south and you will see the offshore islands. The mouth of Somes Sound is not as wide nor as deep as the rest of the fiord. It is only 41 feet deep compared to depths to 157 feet for the main canal. It is said that if the floor at the mouth of the fiord should uplift by 50 feet, there would be another lake on the island. Glacial till and marine deposition has filled the entrance in more recent time.

THE NATIVE ROCK

The point below you, the broad grassy field, is Fernald Point, which is the site of the French Jesuit Mission of 1613, it is believed. The point of land across the narrow entrance to the fiord is Manchester Point, where Abnaki Indians from the Penobscot and Passamaquoddy tribes summered. While on the island, they dug and smoked clams and gathered and dried berries for the long winters.

VIEW FROM FLYING MT.

Unlike fiords of Scandinavia, Somes Sound has two openings, one to the lowlands and the other to the ocean. Fiords have one opening to the sea and a high wall or glacial cirque at the other end. Somes Sound is very deep and narrow between Norumbega Mountain on the east and Flying Mountain, St. Sauveur, and Acadia Mountain on the west.

Continue your climb over Flying Mountain. Your hike will take you over Cadillac granite where short explorations on side trips will provide scratches and chatter marks and also excellent views of Somes Sound.

The descent from the mountain will take you over broken bluffs, great blocks of fractured granite down to a talus deposit of sharp and angular boulders, down further to a till deposit of rounded boulders of all rock types left by the glacier. The broken bluffs at the top and the talus deposit are granite. The till is made up of gravel, sand, clay, and boulders of the area granites, diorites, sedimentary, and Avalonian metamorphic rocks.

THE NATIVE ROCK

The descent takes you to the beach of Valley Cove. In this cove the glacier built up. It tried to clear a way for itself southward, but the igneous rock of Flying Mountain would not give. Eventually, perhaps after thousands of years of trying, the ice poured through both east and west of the mountain rock, through Somes Sound and the Valley.

DESCENT FROM FLYING MT.

THE NATIVE ROCK

Look north up Somes Sound. On the right is Sargent Drive below Norumbega Mountain, named for an Indian legend about a beautiful city that once existed somewhere in the Northeast. Native Americans told early explorers that the name Norumbega meant "quiet water between falls or rapids" and water does plunge down the mountains into the Sound. Historians believe the word may be a corruption of two words that mean "Norse settlement".

On the left is St. Sauveur and Acadia Mountains. Running from ledges between the two mountains is a fresh water stream called Man O'War Brook, where battleships of the 1700's pulled along shore to fill their barrels.

Look north up Somes Sound and then walk to your right around the shore. The point ahead has a beautiful beach made up of the grains of pink feldspar and quartz from Cadillac granite. Examine both the grains and the well-jointed rocks at the shoreline on this point.

VIEW NORTH, SOMES SOUND

THE NATIVE ROCK

This jointing is a natural jointing that we rarely see on the island because the glacier removed the well-jointed areas when it passed over. The spot was perhaps preserved by the uplifting of the ice as it struggled with Flying Mountain before cruising off to the left and right to the south. This spot also was perhaps protected by till that fell out of the glacier as the ice remained and melted. You may be reminded of yeast rolls, big, pink granite yeast rolls that were baked in a pan together. They are covered with barnacles, those rocks below the tide zone, that is. Note also the large blocks of red granite near the shoreline that appear to have been quarried. The rock along the sound has been quarried over the years. (You may return to your car by walking the fire road.)

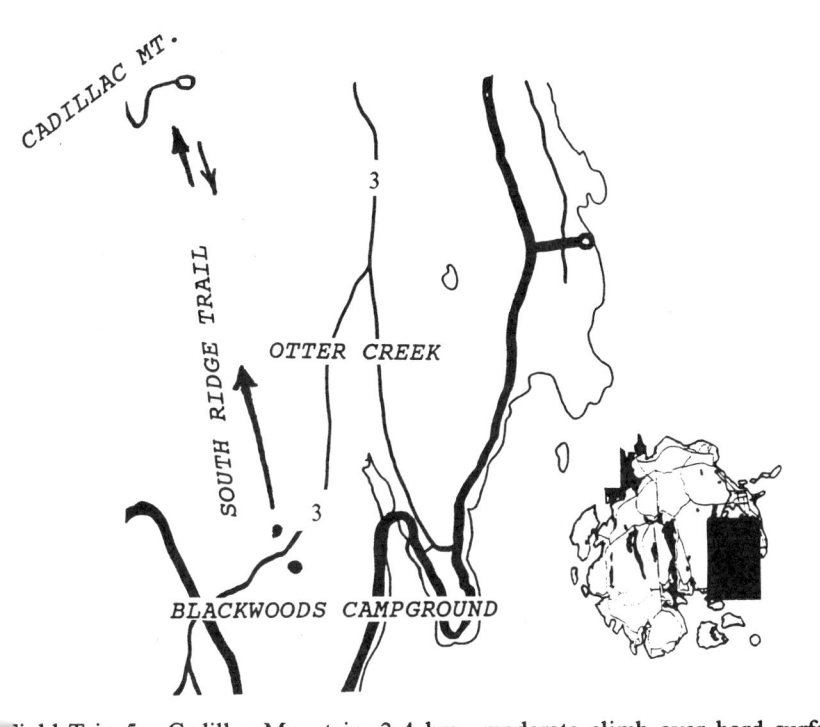

Field Trip 5 - Cadillac Mountain, 3-4 hrs., moderate climb over hard surface and good footing, parking across the road from the entrance to Blackwoods Campground, 4-5 miles of hiking, excellent views of the ocean and island, inland hike to an elevation of 1530 feet, with return the same way down or one of your party could drive your car to the summit of Mt. Cadillac to meet your group on top, look for the wooden sign post and stone steps that mark the start of the South Ridge Trail.

THE NATIVE ROCK

You will hike the South Ridge Trail of Cadillac Mountain to the Summit. The ocean waves eroded shorelines on the mountain slope 13,000-14,000 years ago as the ice receded from the island. The depressed crust filled with the water. An inland sea covered the lower lands of the island. In time the crust rebounded. It uplifted. Old shorelines were uplifted so it is possible today to find beaches and marine deposits on the lowlands and hills. As you climb the South Ridge, you will walk over some of these features.

Continue climbing and enjoy the views as you get up higher. Keep on the look out for the first exposures of the diabase dikes that run in the northwesterly direction. The first presence of them will be a narrow band of black that interrupts the pink granite here and there. Soon enough you will be upon them in all their glory. These dikes belong to a set that cuts its way through the mountain like wide ribbons. They run northwesterly and were formed after the northeasterly dikes. About 200 million years ago, after North America and Africa separated, North America and Europe began to part. In the stretching of the plates as the two moved apart, cracks were formed. Dark magma filled the cracks to repair the damage done to the crust. These dikes are straighter and smoother than the others.

VIEW SOUTH FROM CADILLAC MT. DIKE

THE NATIVE ROCK

The dikes on Cadillac form a giant Y. The lower section soon splits ahead of you. If you look up ahead from the lower section, you can see the black rock reach for the summit where the right side of the Y can be traced over the summit road to the other side of the mountain. On the road to the summit, there are several blasted areas perhaps where this dike continues.

One big saddle pond is called the Featherbed. A section of black dike runs to one side of it. Because of the gray and green lichens that grow on both the pink granite and black dike, many people never see either rock.

It is said that in the 1800's, farmers kept flocks of sheep in the mountain. Every now and then a sheep was lost, supposedly eaten by a wild animal, so a group of men went up the mountain with weapons. They came back to say that they had found a big hole in the mountain from which a giant snake came. They plugged up the hole so the snake could never get out again. It worked! With the hole plugged, no more sheep disappeared! Be sure not to leave the mountain without seeing the snake!

At the Featherbed in a low place on the ridge, the dike is over 6 feet wide. The dike as well as the granite was carved by the glacier. The grip of the ice has made P formations which retain the center filling lines. Explore in this area. There are small pot holes of 6-8 inches across on the ridge. They are the weathered deposits of small inclusions of rock and mineral that may have sunk into the pluton from overlying rock layers. Some of them are filled with soil and others are bare. Some contain small deposits of the green mineral epidote.

There are other saddle ponds in this area which are filled with till and water. They were formed when the glacial ice reached from the U-shaped valleys to this elevation. The ice that built up above this elevation flowed in a different direction. While the ice in lower elevations flowed more N-S, the ice in the higher elevations shifted more W-E. The saddle ponds were cut when the ice shifted. The higher ice flowed over the land-locked lower ice.

In the area of the Featherbed and other nearby saddle ponds, there are chatter marks as big as the rims of dinner plates.

On the left hand side of the upper section of the Y dike, there is a good exposure of a pink dike within the pink granite. This is probably a fill line through which the granite body filled itself when it formed millions of years ago deep within the earth. These fill lines are not unlike the center lines of rifts through which magma upwells in the ocean floors.

THE NATIVE ROCK

The rocks on Cadillac are weathered, stained, and covered with lichen. If you have difficulty spotting the dikes, be patient, therefore, and look for differences in texture and shape. The dikes are smoother than the grained granites, and their jointed and broken surfaces are more angular. Enjoy the fresh air and view! Here's hoping your day to climb the South Ridge is sunny and clear!

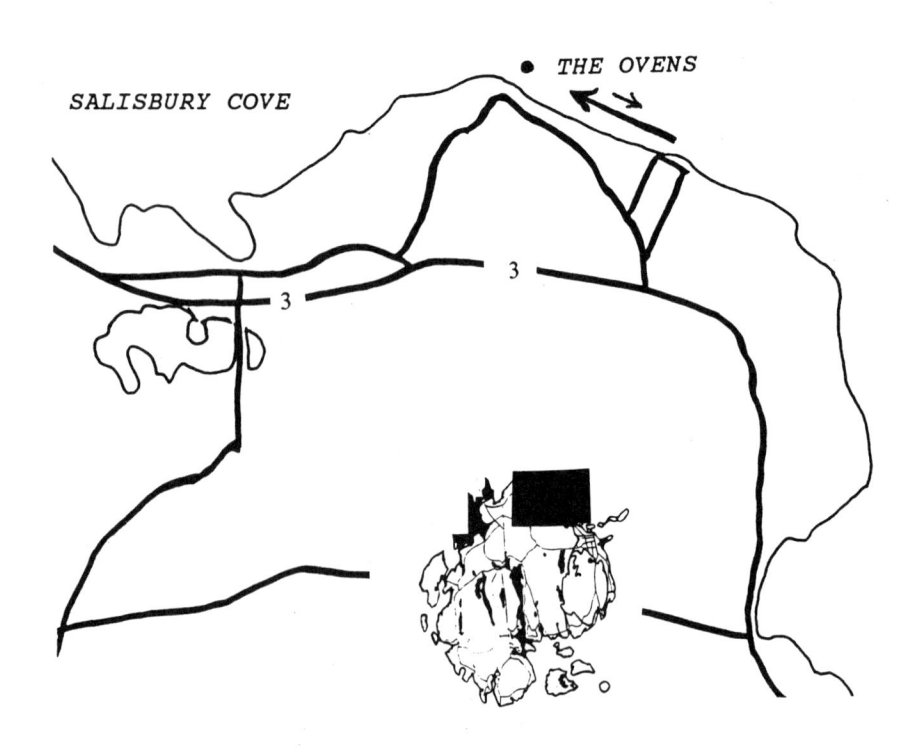

Field Trip 6 - The Ovens, 2-3 hrs., easy walking, but uneven footing at times over cobbles and boulders and shingles, low tide a must, under 3 miles, parking along the roadside, no public road to the shore.

Ask permission before crossing private land to the shore or take a boat to this site. Look across the Narrows to the mainland in the north. Walk to the left or northwest. The sandstones are worn from the Bar Harbor Series sedimentary rock. An outcropping or two can be seen at low tide. Walk about one mile. On your right, the layers can be seen in the cliffs.

There are numerous fault lines in them. These show the slippage of the Bar Harbor Series under the diorite and Avalonian rocks to the northwest.

THE NATIVE ROCK

Two very prominent black layers can be identified, each about 4 inches wide and separated by a wide greenish layer. They are discolored so the bands can not always be spotted easily. Be patient, and you will spot them sooner or later as you walk northwestward. At the time of their formation, the land mass was approaching the equator about 375 million years ago.

What was going on at that time to result in the black layers and the thick green zone? The two black layers received decayed matter while the green layers between them were tinted by living matter. Perhaps the two carbon layers were zones in an ancient sea just north and south of the equator while the large body of chlorite layers was deposited at the equator. Perhaps the two black layers relate to a period of time during which sediments filled the ocean floor slowly along with large amounts of decayed vegetation and sea life while the wide layer relates to a period of time when there was a great amount of land erosion that covered the living matter on the ocean floor quickly.

As the cliff becomes higher, note that a second rock type is deposited on the first. The rock shows ash and broken fragments and a material called felsite by some geologists and rhyolite by others. The rock above is yellowish and reddish brown. The beach stones include this material too. The wave-worn pieces appear smooth but still angular. Felsite and rhyolite are igneous rocks that cooled in layers.

Although it does contain concretions like those found at Seawall Picnic Area on the southwest side of the island, geologists do not place this deposit with the eruptions of the Cranberry Island Series. It may have formed before or after the Bar Harbor Series. Currently, it is believed by some geologists to be a part of the Bar Harbor Series.

Look closely at the concretions which have eroded centers of a greenish color. They are not unlike weathered limonite which has a greenish end product. Many of these have a small deposit of iron minerals near them. Perhaps iron-rich rock from the volcano fell into the hot magma. In a natural process, it may have become smelted, producing a lump of pig iron and the residual greenish material. Concretions like these often contain fossils so perhaps the greenish material was once a plant or sea animal.

Soon you will spot the sea caves and the natural wave-worn arch. Near the arch you will see a part of the cliff which has fallen onto the beach. The newly exposed rock is lighter in color. In time it will weather to reddish browns. Do not go into the caves. The rock is unstable and may fall on you.

THE NATIVE ROCK

SEA CAVE

Spot the colorful pigments on the cliffs. One area is as bright as an artist's palette. Water that seeps through the rock dissolves and carries bright yellow, red, orange, purple, and green colors to the beach below. These can best be seen on a rainy day.

SEA-CARVED ARCH

THE NATIVE ROCK

Spot the vertical fault that remains opened by about 8-10 inches. Both sides of the vertical fault are white from a build-up of minerals, which were deposited from water, either water that seeped into the earth or water that shot out of the earth.

VERTICAL FAULTLINE

The shoreline over which you have crossed has taken you out of the bedrock of the Bar Harbor Series. You will see the downfolding where the Bar Harbor Series disappear under the volcanics. This could be a former trench or subduction zone. Walking along northwesterly, you will soon pass into Salisbury Cove and there the bedrock becomes the Avalonian metamorphic.

To reach Salisbury Cove on foot would require at least another hour of walking to return to your car. Then you can drive to the cove and walk to the right of the cove about 600 feet past some diorite to Avalonian metamorphic. You will see a faultline of broken and twisted stone, a rather unimpressive faultline, that has been traced through Hamilton's Pond. It disappears in the area of Northeast Creek. This line continues across the island passing through Town Hill somewhere in the vicinity of Clark's Cove and Indian Point, it is believed. Avalonian rock appears throughout the northwestern part of the island.

THE NATIVE ROCK

A Word from the Author

The Island of Mount Desert and the landscape of the Northeast matches the description of Plato's Atlantis; however, several other locations around the world qualify on many points as well. More study is needed: More features, both geologic and cultural, need to be found.

The author encourages readers to become familiar with Plato's <u>Timaeus</u> and <u>Critias</u>, the stories that provide the details of an Atlantean civilization. Maine's people, especially those who hike the coastline, rivers, and mountains are more likely to know the unique characteristics of their state. Explore! Test ideas and report the results.

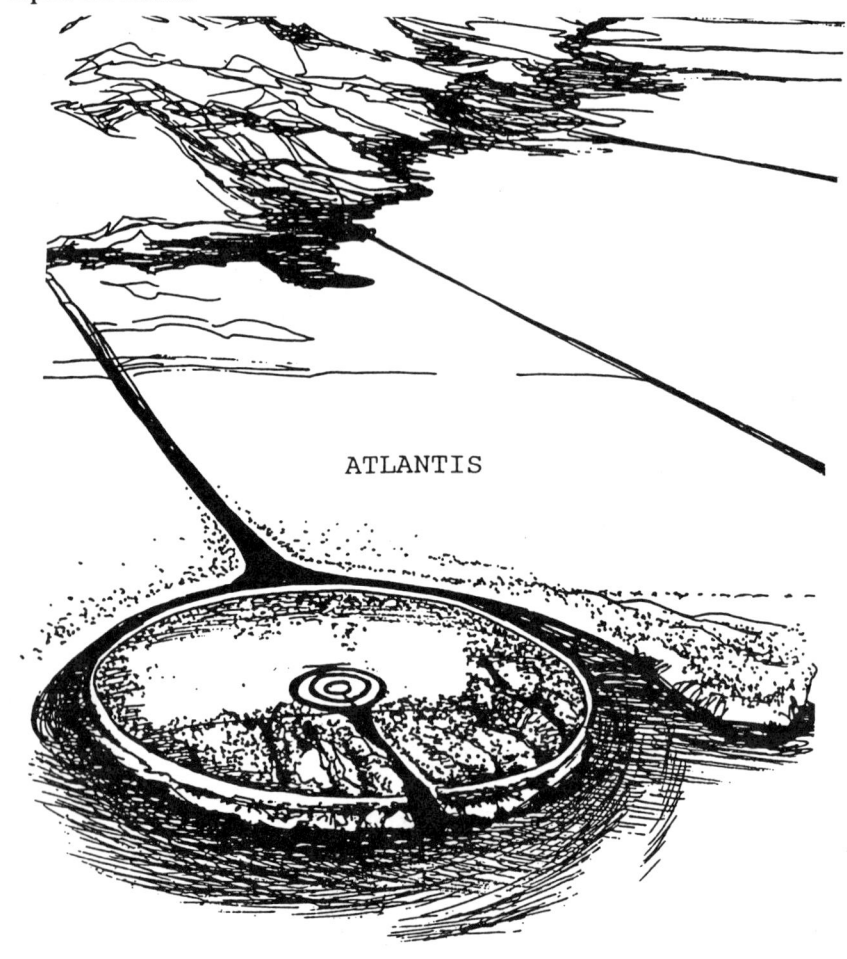

ATLANTIS

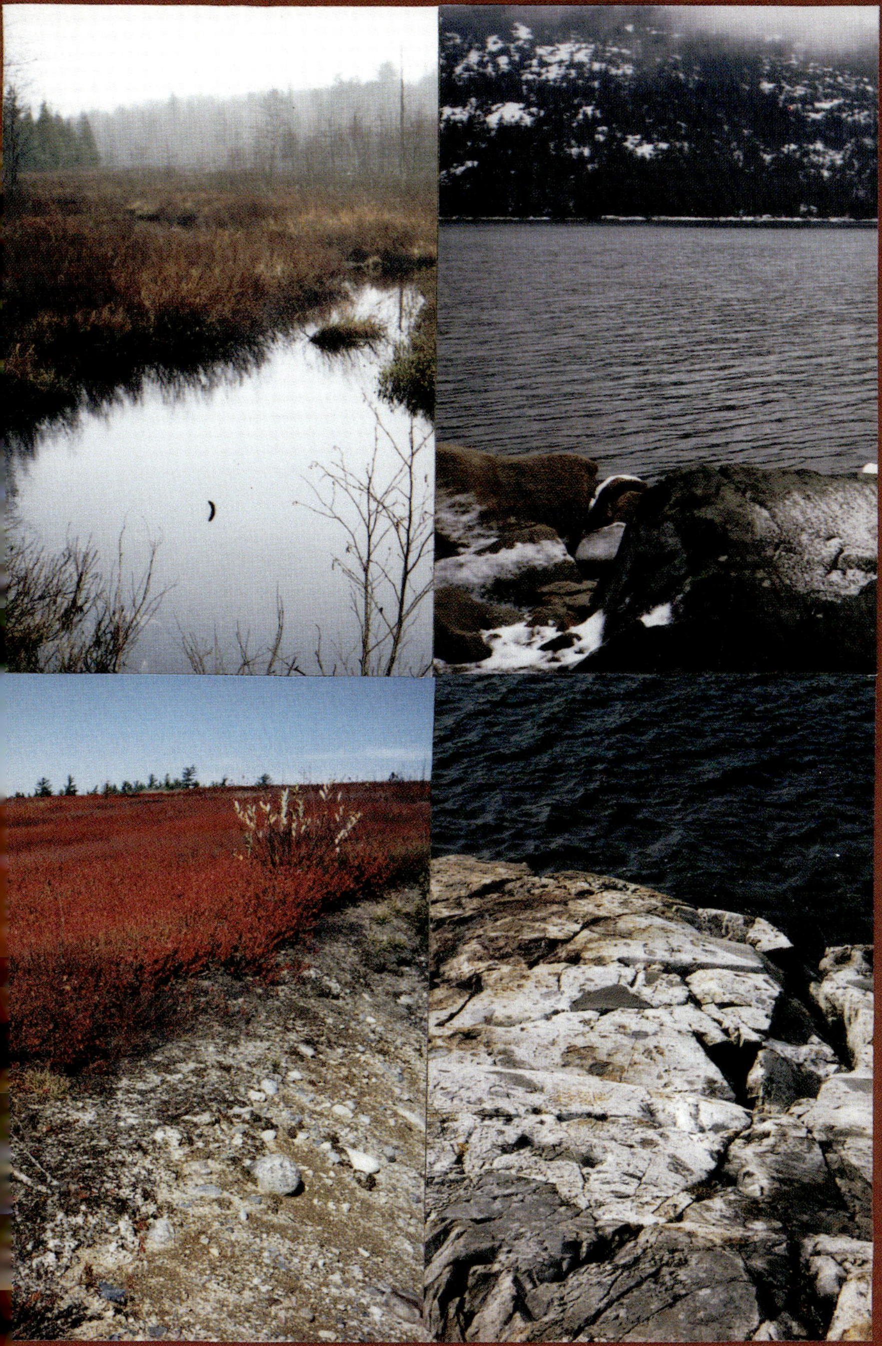

ATLANTEAN FEATURES

Top Left: SOMESVILLE WETLAND
              Circular zone of wet soils, north of Somesville Village

Top Right: SOMES SOUND FROM SARGENT DRIVE
              Channel 5 nautical miles long between Norumbega and
              Acadia mountains

Bottom Left: BLUEBERRY BARRENS ON THE MAINLAND
              Rt. 1 into Machias, Maine, a part of a vast glacial plain

Bottom Right: SHATTER ZONE, GREAT HEAD
              East of Sand Beach, Acadia National Park, "the wall of Atlantis"

THE NATIVE ROCK

The Lofty Country, Atlantis

A Description of Mount Desert Island

An interesting description was written (360 B.C.) by the Greek philosopher Plato in the dialogues of <u>Timaeus</u> and <u>Critias</u> about an island Atlantis in the Atlantic Ocean. He wrote that the account "though strange" was "certainly true." Although written over 2300 years ago, the story was older, having been handed down several generations. Plato said that the island of Atlantis had been destroyed 9000 years before his account, which amounts to 11-12,000 years ago. _{Jowett}

The description of Atlantis seems remarkably similar to Mount Desert Island and northeastern Maine and New Brunswick. You can decide for yourself, for following is Plato's description with a geologic comparison to the Northeast.

Two questions are asked. Had the Coast of Maine been known and remembered some 2500 - 3000 years ago? Had Plato's sources related a description of a vast glacial plain and theorized a mighty people had once lived on the land to explain its geologic and glacial features? Or had there, indeed, been a perfected City of Atlantis and plain of the Continent of Atlantis, populated by hard-working Atlanteans who lived 12,000 years ago?

> The account is told to an early Greek, Solon, by an Egyptian priest who said that "the Atlantic was navigable; and there was an island situated in front of the straits...called the pillars of Heracles..." _{Jowett}

> Another translation describes "it is in all nine thousand years since a general war...was declared between those who dwelt without and those who dwelt within the Pillars of Heracles." _{Taylor}

The Straits of Gibraltar were called the "Pillars of Heracles" in ancient times, but ideas as to the location of Atlantis today include not only through the straits into the Atlantic but within the straits in the Mediterranean Sea.

> Atlantis was an island that was reached before an "opposite continent which surrounded the true ocean; for this sea which is within the Straits of Heracles is only a harbour, having a narrow entrance, but that other is a real sea." _{Jowett}

THE NATIVE ROCK

"Atlantis... was once...an island larger than Libya and Asia [northern Africa and Turkey] together; it has now been engulfed by earthquakes and is the source of the impassable mud which prevents navigators from this quarter from advancing through the straits into the open ocean." Taylor

Over 11,000 years ago, there was glacial ice over most of North America in the higher latitudes. The ice had receded 13,000-14,000 years ago from the area of MDI, but ice in northern Maine and Canada was still in place. The land of Mount Desert Island and surrounding area at that time was in a rebound mode, land lifting out of the sea due to the release from the weight of ice. Studies in Scandinavia show that the earth's crust can lift as fast as half a foot a year when a glacier recedes. This uplifted land may have presented a continent of the dimensions described for Atlantis.

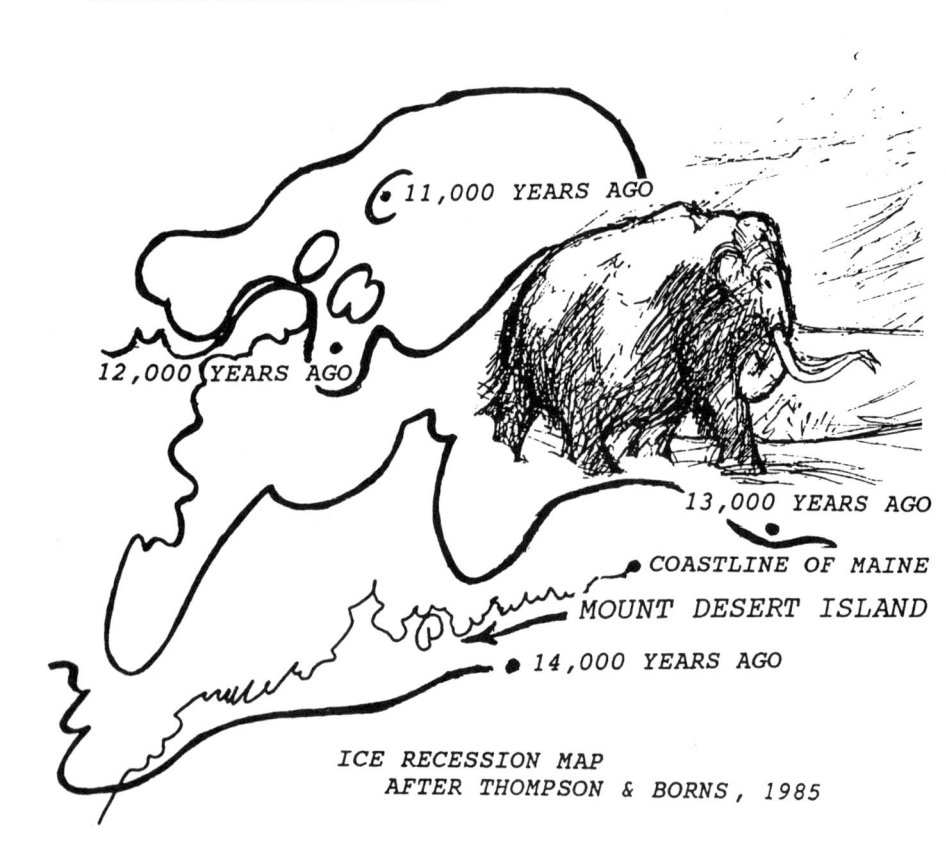

11,000 YEARS AGO

12,000 YEARS AGO

13,000 YEARS AGO

COASTLINE OF MAINE
MOUNT DESERT ISLAND

14,000 YEARS AGO

ICE RECESSION MAP
AFTER THOMPSON & BORNS, 1985

THE NATIVE ROCK

The Egyptian priest told Solon that the pre-Greeks had been at war with the Atlanteans when followed "violent earthquakes and floods."
Jowett

The earthquake had a large scale effect upon the earth, for while Atlantis was destroyed, the pre-Greek culture was not spared. "To begin with, the Acropolis was not then as it is now [Plato's time]. At present it has been washed bare of soil by one night of extraordinary floods in which an earthquake and the third terrible deluge before that of Deucalion befell together."
Taylor

The "violent earthquakes and floods" over 11,000 years ago may have come from glacial ice that released meltwater from shifting, land-locked ice masses to the north. There are mountains to the northwest, including Mount Katahdin, which are glacially scoured. With the floods, mud would have washed over the island. On Mount Desert Island there are deposits of steeply inclined beds of stone, gravel, sand, silt, clay and mud that were placed by violent water. One deposit in the Somesville area contains limestone that came from over a hundred miles to the north.

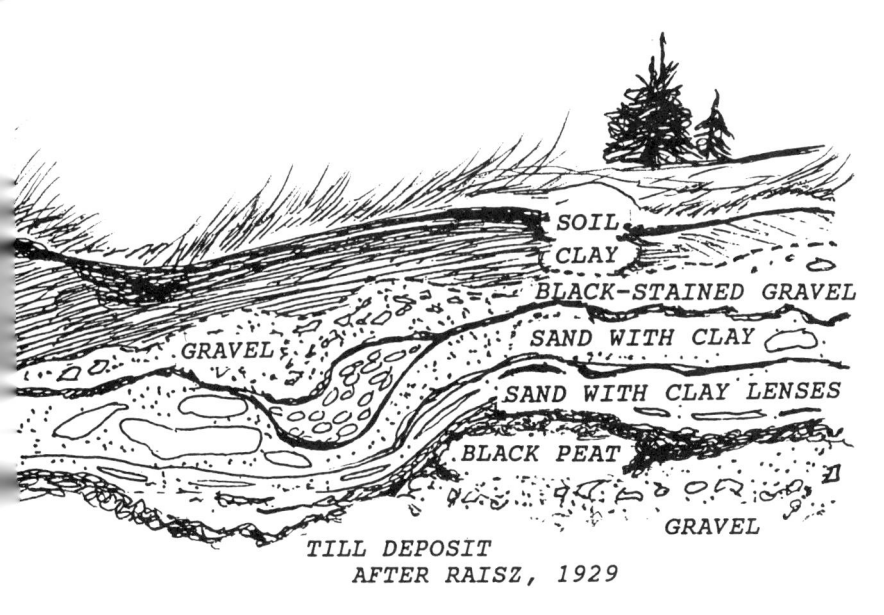

TILL DEPOSIT
AFTER RAISZ, 1929

THE NATIVE ROCK

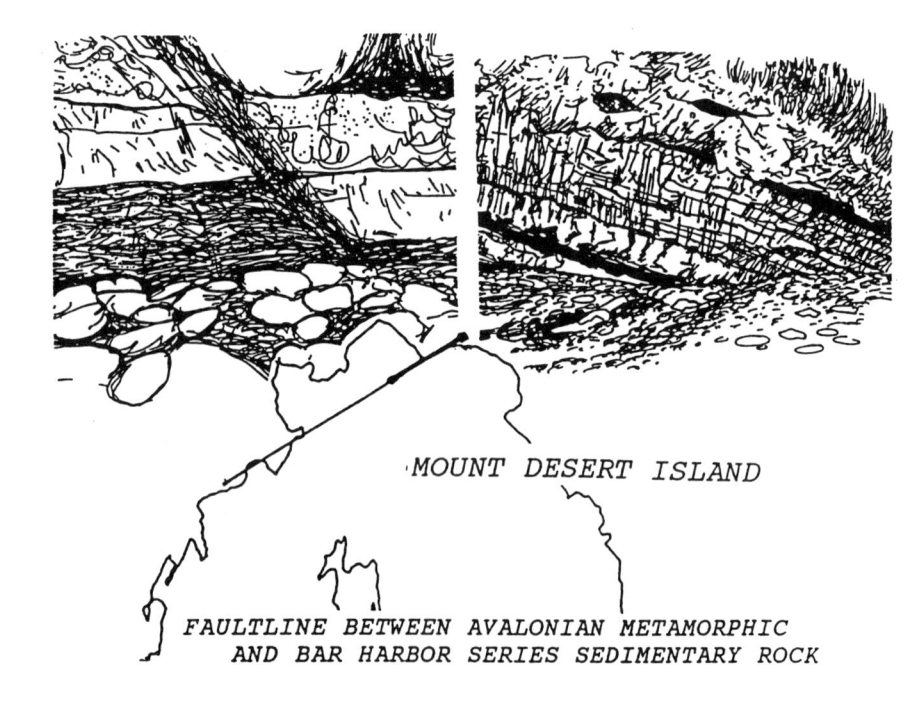

MOUNT DESERT ISLAND

FAULTLINE BETWEEN AVALONIAN METAMORPHIC AND BAR HARBOR SERIES SEDIMENTARY ROCK

The faultlines across the northwestern part of MDI indicate earthquake activity if not the subsidence of the northwestern area of the island. At the Ovens in Salisbury Cove, Bar Harbor Series sedimentary rock layers are fractured in numerous places. A subduction zone shows the sedimentary series dipping beneath the Avalonian metamorphic and diorite sill formations. Furthermore earthquakes in North America could have sent tidal waves onto European and North African shores.

In the middle of the island of Atlantis there was a smaller island about 11-12 nautical miles across. This description is somewhat confusing when you read it for the first time, for not only is there an island within a larger island or continent, but on the smaller island, there is a city which is divided into circular zones of land and sea and these land areas are referred to islands and islets as well.

THE NATIVE ROCK

On the smaller island, a canal was cut that was five nautical miles long (all miles given here are nautical miles which correspond to stadia, 1 nautical mile = 10 stadia), 100 feet deep, and 300 feet wide. The canal led from the sea to the center of the island where the city was built. The city was about 2 1/2 miles across and was circular in shape. In the very center of the city was a hill where the palace was built that was 1/2 mile across. Around that was a canal about 1/10 of a mile, then a circle of land 2/10 of a mile, then a canal 2/10 of a mile, then a circle of land 3/10 of a mile, then a canal 3/10 of a mile.

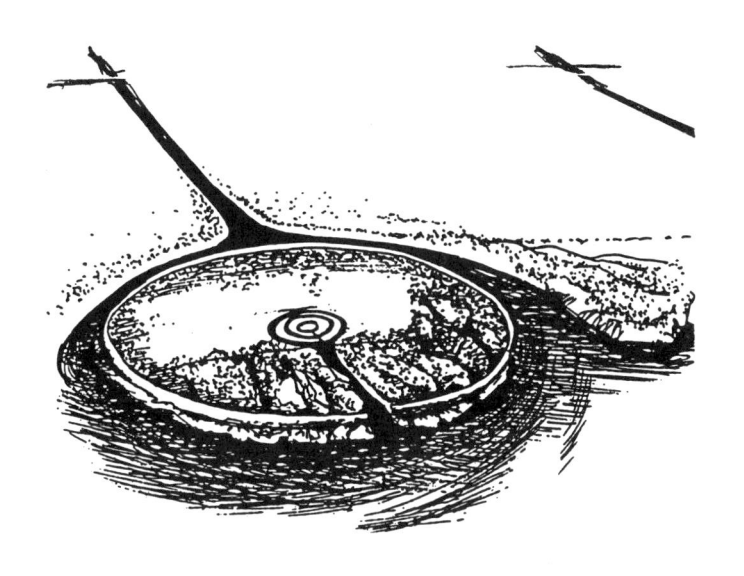

AS DESCRIBED BY PLATO

The description for these zones is not given here, but if you would like to read this for yourself, ask for Plato's <u>Critias</u> at your library. For this comparison, content concerns geology, but Plato's account gives details about the people, both the ancient pre-Greeks and the Atlanteans. Indeed, the first half of the dialogue is about Greece and its destruction during the same time of earthquakes and floods. The account is the Greek equivalent of the Biblical flood.

THE NATIVE ROCK

The zones of the "ancient metropolis" were given access to the sea; "they bored a canal of 300 feet in width and one hundred feet in depth and fifty stadia in length...making a passage from the sea..." Jowett

"By the sea, in the center of the island, there was a plain, said to have been the most beauteous of all such plains and very fertile..." Taylor

At the center of the city, a "fortified hill" was surrounded by "alternate rings of sea and land, smaller and greater, one within the other...two such round wheels, as we may call them, of earth and three of sea from the very center of the island, at uniform distances..." Taylor

"They first bridged the rings of sea round their original home, thus making themselves a road from and to their palace." Taylor

"They began on the seaside by cutting a canal to the outermost ring, fifty stadia long, three hundred feet broad, and a hundred feet deep; the 'ring' could now be entered from the sea by this canal like a port, as the opening they had made would admit the largest of the vessels." Taylor

SOMES SOUND

VIEW SOUTH OVER MOUNT DESERT ISLAND

The measurements of the canal from the sea are similar to those of Somes Sound of five nautical miles long, 900 feet wide at its entrance, 41 feet deep at its mouth where there is a buildup of till and marine deposition, and 157 feet in the main canal. It is possible that Somes Sound had a more even distribution of till at one time. If a violent flood approached MDI from the north, it could have realigned the sediments in the bottom of Somes Sound as well as widened the canal.

THE NATIVE ROCK

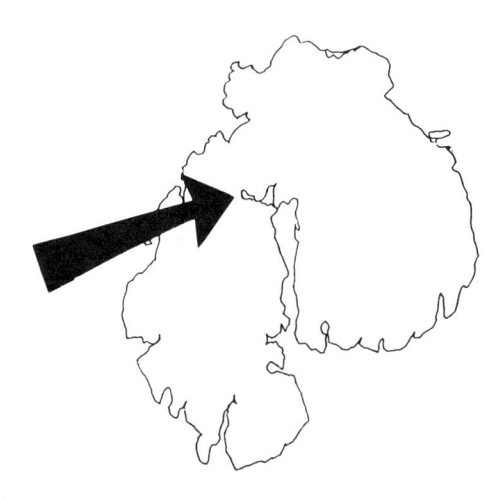

The "ancient metropolis" would be located at Somesville. In a radius of 2 1/2 nautical miles about the head of the sound, there is a deposit of rich organic soil which geologists report as a flat and wet area that results when basins are filled in slowly over time. Elsewhere on the island, the rich organic soils occupy depressions that were once pond and lake basins.

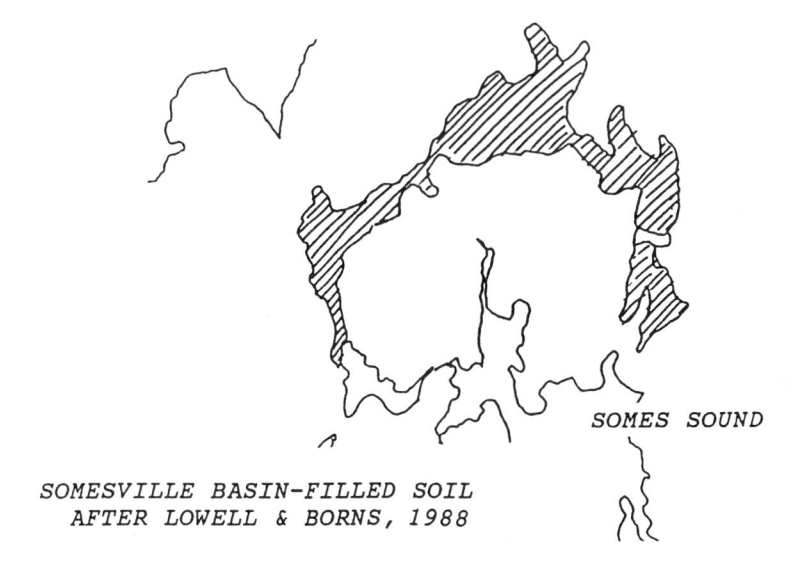

SOMES SOUND

SOMESVILLE BASIN-FILLED SOIL
AFTER LOWELL & BORNS, 1988

THE NATIVE ROCK

Just north of the Somesville deposit, there is the northwestern fault line where the Bar Harbor Series of sedimentary folds down under the Avalonian and diorite. Although this faultline has only been traced a short distance, it is believed to extend across the island's northwest border.

> "The stone which was used in the work they quarried from underneath the centre island... One kind was white, another black, and a third red..."
> Jowett

> "The stone, black, white, and red, they quarried beneath the whole central islet and outer and inner rings..."
> Taylor

Mount Desert Island's pink granite, the dark diabase and gabbro, the diorite and white quartz all qualify as stone which can be found today in Somesville.

The story described many fine features of the city that parallel those found in Egypt and Greece. The Egyptian priest telling the story may have been trying to make a point, a point made to him by an early Atlantean: Atlantean culture equaled if not surpassed that which was found in the Mediterranean. Was someone boasting? Was someone exaggerating? Or did truly such a culture exist 12,000 years ago?

The center hill about which the city was developed was only 1/2 mile across. Under it the stone was quarried for the city so in time, perhaps, the hill was cut away as more buildings were constructed. There are many small hills under 200 feet high within the circle of the rich, organic soil deposit that surround Somesville, but the area for the most part makes up a lowland that covers the northern part of the island. No search for an ancient city has been conducted.

> At a distance from the city there was "a wall which began at the sea and went all round: this was everywhere distant fifty stadia from the largest zone or harbour, and enclosed the whole..."
> Jowett

THE NATIVE ROCK

SHATTER ZONE

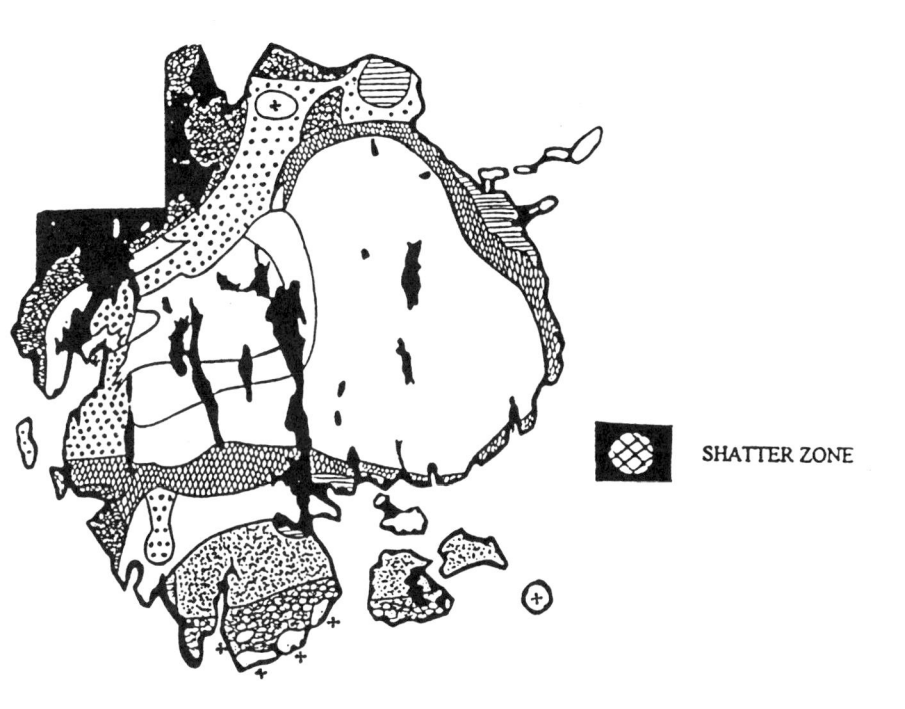

"When one had passed the three outer harbors, a wall ran all round, starting at the sea, at a uniform distance of fifty stadia from the greatest ring and its harbor, returning on itself at the mouth of the canal from the sea. This wall was completely filled by a multitude of closely set houses, and the large harbor and canal were constantly crowded by merchant vessels and their passengers arriving from all quarters, whose vast numbers occasioned incessant shouting, clamor, and general uproar, day and night."
Taylor

The wall in this passage refers to the outer shoreline of the island. From the center of the island where the city was built there was a distance of about five miles to the shoreline in all directions. MDI is bordered by a shatter zone on its north, east, and south, and shortly after the glacial ice receded and the land rebounded, the contact zone may have appeared like a cement wall in which broken stone was added. Today's view of it is obscured by the weathering and staining it shows at its surface. Some of the giant blocks within the granite and diorite matrix may have perplexed the early observers to these shores.

THE NATIVE ROCK

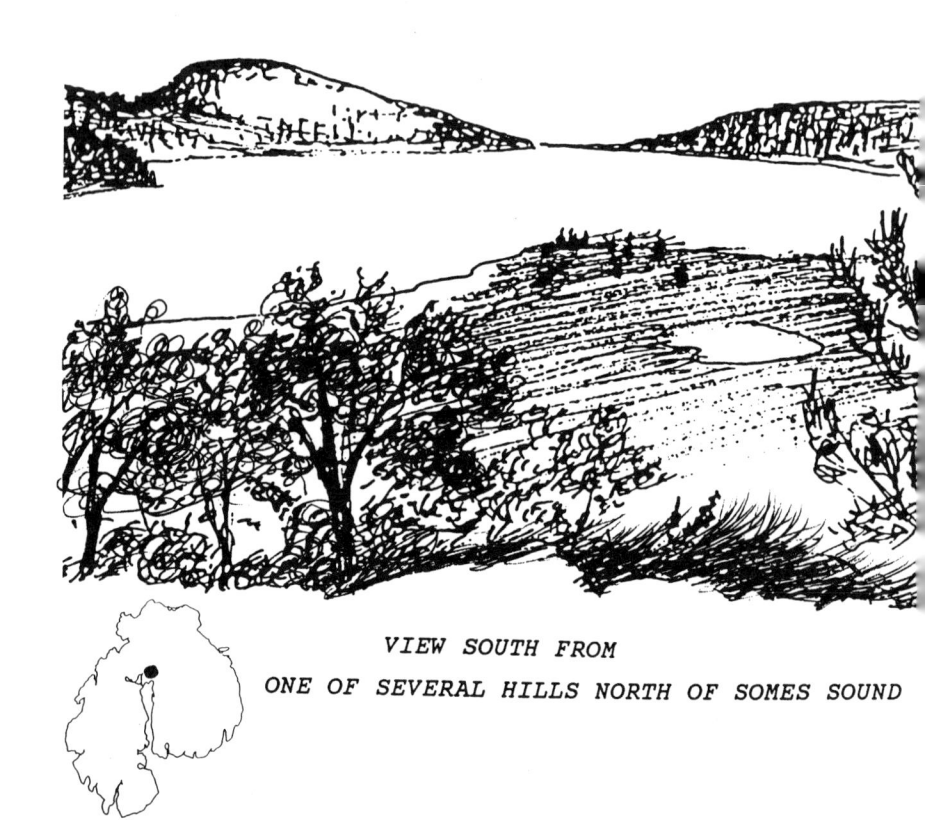

VIEW SOUTH FROM ONE OF SEVERAL HILLS NORTH OF SOMES SOUND

Glacial till and erratics would have perplexed them while polished stone and colored rock would have been valuable to them in construction.

The Egyptian priest who is the story teller of Atlantis lived about 450-500 B.C. He may have visited North America, himself, or he may have talked with people who had. His description compares well with MDI.

> "The whole country was...very lofty and precipitous on the side of the sea..." while there was a plain immediately surrounding and to the north of the city in an "oblong shape, extending in one direction three thousand stadia, but across the centre inland it was two thousand stadia."
>
> Jowett

THE NATIVE ROCK

"...[I] must do my best to recall the general character of the territory," wrote Plato, "and its organization. To begin with, the district as a whole, so I have heard, was of great elevation, and its coast precipitous, but all round the city was a plain, enclosing it and itself enclosed in turn by mountain ranges which came right down to the sea. The plain itself was smooth, level, and of a generally oblong shape; it stretched for three thousand stadia in one direction, and, at its center, for two thousand inland from the coast. All through the island this level district faced the south and was thus screened from the cold northerly winds. In those times it was famous for its encircling mountains, which were more numerous, huge, and beautiful than any that exist today. These mountains contained numerous villages with a wealthy population, besides rivers, lakes, and meadows which provided plentiful sustenance for all sorts of animals, wild or domestic, and timber of different kinds in quantities amply sufficient for manufactures of every type." Taylor

"From the first, it [the plain] was naturally quadrangular, oblong, and nearly rectangular; departures from that shape had been corrected by the carrying of a fosse round it. As to the depth, breadth, and length of this fosse, it sounds incredible that any work of human hands should be so vast by comparison with other achievements of the kind, but I have to tell the tale as I heard it. It has been dug to the depth of a hundred feet, had everywhere a stadium in breadth, and as it was carried completely round the plain, its length came to ten thousand stadia." Taylor

The "whole country" refers to the whole of Atlantis, of which the island domain of the city was only a part. To understand where the whole might be, we need to look to the mainland for an area 200 nautical miles inland and 300 long. Immediately to our north there is a glacial outwash plain. On a part of it, the sand quarries of Lamoine provide construction materials. To the north and east, there are blueberry barrens of Hancock and Washington Counties, which we know are glacial soils. To the far north of Maine there are the potato fields of Aroostock County. Much of Penobscot County between them is rolling hills, but that is not perhaps what it was just after the glacier receded. From the

THE NATIVE ROCK

Penobscot River to the St. John River in New Brunswick, there may have been one vast level plain of outwash material.

West of the Penobscot River there are mountains including Mount Katahdin, north of which the glacial sheet may have built up. These could be the mountains that protected the plain from the north, which might have appeared as a sea of ice. With ice to the northeast as well, the exposed and uplifted outwash plain of the glacier may have been the plain of Atlantis.

> "The surrounding mountains were celebrated for their number and size and beauty..."
> Jowett

The beauty of the "lofty and precipitous country to the side of the sea" would be the mountains of MDI, and the "surrounding mountains", those in western and northern Maine. They are celebrated for their number, size, and beauty! The lakes, meadows, and forests remain wonderful memories for all who see them! The precipitous coast, the rugged, rockbound coast of Maine!

> The plain north of the city "was fashioned by nature and by the labours of many generations..." Around the plain was a ditch that "was excavated to the depth of a hundred feet, and its breadth was a stadium everywhere; it was carried round the whole of the plain, and was ten thousand stadia in length."
> Jowett

It was recognized that the plain was formed by nature, and that it had been cultivated or developed by generations of people. A part of the circular ditch, which had a length of 1000 miles, could have been the St. Lawrence Seaway in Quebec, Canada. It is suggested that a body of water encircled the land which was 200 miles inland from the coast and 300 miles long. Lake Champlain in New York connected to the St. Lawrence River, which formed an arm of the sea which extended southward toward the Atlantic Ocean 12,000 years ago.

The smaller island of 11-12 miles in diameter (Mount Desert Island) was south of the plain. Within the territory from the Penobscot River to the St. John, the people of the Abnaki Nation lived. This was their domain about 3000 years ago. It is questionable, but there may have been earlier people on the coast 5000 years ago. But 12,000 years ago?

THE NATIVE ROCK

The ditch received water from the mountains, where "straight canals of a hundred feet in width were cut...through the plain, and again let off into the ditch leading to the sea..." Jowett

"It [the fosse or ditch] received the watercourses which came down from the mountains, made the tour of the plain, meeting the city in both directions, and was thence allowed to discharge into the sea." Taylor

"Beyond the city, straight canals of some hundred feet in width, terminated once more at the fosse on the seaside, were drawn across the plain, with a distance of a hundred stadia between every two. They were used for the floating of timber down to the town from the mountains and the conveyance by boat of natural produce generally, oblique channels of cross-communication being cut from these canals to one another and the city." Taylor

The canals may be the numerous rivers and streams that run throughout Maine, including the Kennebec, Penobscot and Machias rivers, which were used for log drives as recently as the 1970's. This description tells of the area before the floods and earthquakes that destroyed it. If great amounts of icy water and masses of frozen ice broke from the northern glaciers and washed over the land, it would have certainly destroyed these features before it destroyed the city on its southern border.

Also mentioned in the writings (not quoted here) besides horses were two other animals, elephants and bulls. The mastodon and mammoth were common in North America until the receding of the glacier and the arrival of Europeans and Mediterraneans. Remains of mammoths have been found in glacial moraines. Horses were also found here until the same period of time. The bull could have been the bull moose.

Men have sought Atlantis for thousands of years with only Plato's description to go on! An island as beautiful as Mount Desert Island can not be forgotten!

The glorious skies! The moods of the ocean! The carpeted forest! The celebrated mountains! The lofty country! The quarried rock!

THE NATIVE ROCK

MAMMOTH

MASTADON

Were there Mediterranean people who traveled to North America to trade 2,500-3000 years ago? Did they decide that a culture, the Atlantean, must have thrived thousands of years earlier to explain the perplexing talus, erratics, shatter zone and glacial plain?

Plato's account suggest a city and surrounding countryside where canals were built and maintained in geometric perfection. From the exposed glacial outwash plain was such a work completed 12,000 years ago? Was there a large population of people who maintained the rebounding land before the melting front of glacial ice?

THE NATIVE ROCK

Acadia National Park and Mount Desert Island, Maine! Is our celebrated coastline the re-creation of our God?

Should we ask yet a third question? Is it just a coincidence that Plato's Atlantis and Mount Desert Island share the same geological description?

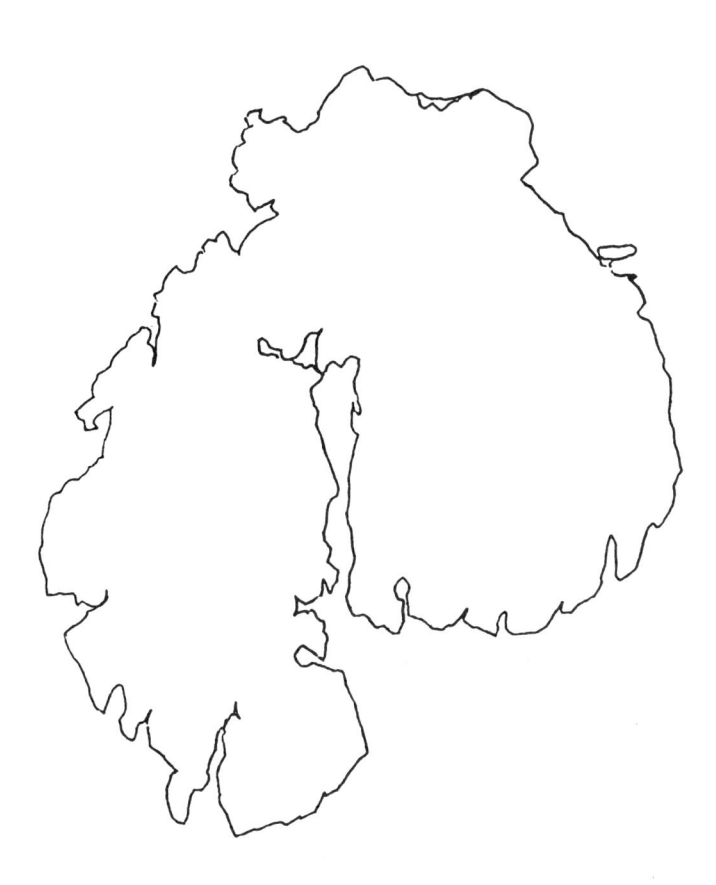

THE NATIVE ROCK

Island of Atlantis	**Island of Mount Desert**
11-12 nautical miles in diameter	10-11 nautical miles in diameter
Channel from the sea on southern border to center island: 5 nautical miles long, 100 ft. deep, 300 ft. wide	Somes Sound from southern border to center island: 5 nautical miles long, 41 ft. deep at entrance and 157 ft. deepest, 900-2500 ft. in width
Red, black, white quarried rock used for building and decoration	Pink Cadillac granite, black diabase, diorite and quartz found at Somesville
City of Atlantis on zones of land and sea, 2 1/2 nautical miles across	Somesville surrounded by wetland and soil deposits that indicate a circular basin, 2 1/2 nautical miles across
Plain around and to the north of the city	Lowland about Somesville and glacial plain to its north
Steep and precipitous coastal border	Cliffs on both Ocean and Sea Cliff Drives and rugged coast of Maine
Plain north of island, 200 nautical miles inland by 300 nautical miles in length	Glacial outwash plain in Eastern Maine and New Brunswick
Continent of Atlantis surrounded by channel on the north, east and west which received meltwater from ice in far northern mountains	State of Maine and Province of New Brunswick surrounded by the St. Lawrence River and the Champlain Sea on the north, east and west 12,000 years ago
Mountains to the north shield plain from winter storms; mountains continue to the sea	Mountains in the north and west of Maine, including Mt. Katahdin

THE NATIVE ROCK

Island of Atlantis	Island of Mount Desert
N-S running canals maintained by industrious Atlanteans	N-S running rivers and streams meandering throughout Maine and New Brunswick
Stone wall around the island, everywhere 5 nautical miles from its center city	Shatter zone on the north, east and south of MDI, 4-5 nautical miles from centrally located Somesville
Destructive floods and earthquakes	Evidence of flood deposits in Somesville and of earthquake activity and subsidence of the northwestern border of the island at the Ovens, Salisbury Cove
Located in the Atlantic	Located in the Atlantic

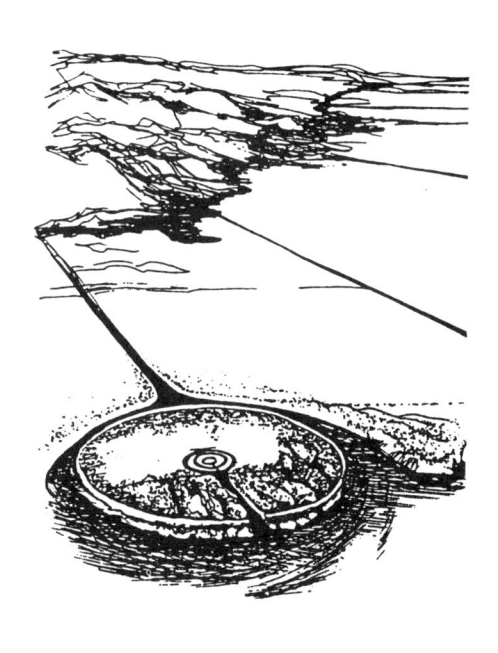

THE NATIVE ROCK

References

1. Erwin J. Raisz, <u>The Scenery of Mount Desert Island: Its Origin and Development</u>, New York: Academy of Sciences, 1929

2. Carleton A. Chapman, <u>The Geology of Mount Desert Island, Maine</u>, Ann Arbor: Edward Brothers, Inc., 1962

3. Richard A. Gilmore, Carleton A. Chapman, Thomas V. Lowell, Harold W. Borns, Jr., Maine Geological Survey, <u>The Geology of Mount Desert Island</u>, Augusta: Maine Department of Conservation: Walter A. Anderson, State Geologist, 1988

4. David L. Kendall, <u>Glaciers & Granite</u>, Camden, Maine, Down East Books, 1987

5. Chet Raymo and Maureen Raymo, <u>Written in Stone</u>, Old Saybrook, Connecticut, The Globe and Pequot Press, 1989

6. David Grene, <u>The History, Herodotus</u>, Chicago: The University of Chicago Press, 1987

7. Benjamin Jowett, <u>The Dialogues of Plato,</u> Oxford University Press, 1893 and Liveright Publishing Co., 1927: New York

8. Edith Hamilton and Huntingon Cairns, <u>Plato, The Collected Dialogues,</u> Princeton, Princeton University Press, 1961 and 1989
Translator: A. E. Taylor, <u>Critias</u>, 1929